Schooling Poor Minority Children

New Segregation in the Post-*Brown* Era

Martha R. Bireda

ROWMAN & LITTLEFIELD EDUCATION

A division of
ROWMAN & LITTLEFIELD PUBLISHERS, INC.
Lanham • New York • Toronto • Plymouth, UK

Published by Rowman & Littlefield Education
A division of Rowman & Littlefield Publishers, Inc.
A wholly owned subsidary of The Rowman & Littlefield Publishing Group, Inc.
4501 Forbes Boulevard, Suite 200, Lanham, Maryland 20706
http://www.rowmaneducation.com

Estover Road, Plymouth PL6 7PY, United Kingdom

British Library Cataloguing in Publication Information Available

Library of Congress Cataloging-in-Publication Data

Bireda, Martha R.
  Schooling poor minority children : new segregation in the post-Brown era /
Martha R. Bireda
    p. cm.
  Includes bibliographical references
  ISBN 978-1-60709-882-9 (cloth : alk. paper) — ISBN 978-1-60709-883-6 (pbk.
: alk. paper) — ISBN 978-1-60709-884-3 (electronic)
  1. Children of minorities—Education. 2. Children with social disabilities—
Education—United States. 3. Multicultural education. 4. Segregation in
education—Government policy. I. Title.
LC3993.9.B57 2011
370.117—dc22
                                                                2010053893

∞™ The paper used in this publication meets the minimum requirements of
American National Standard for Information Sciences—Permanence of Paper
for Printed Library Materials, ANSI/NISO Z39.48-1992.

Printed in the United States of America

To my teachers, who always held the highest expectations for me, especially: Mrs. Evelyn Thompson Lawrence, Mrs. Lorene Bailey, Mrs. Essie Mae Clemons, Mrs. Esther Dailey, and Mr. Charles Holden

Contents

Preface

I am a product of segregated schools in the South. I am one of the children on whose behalf the fight to desegregate public schools was waged. In 1951, the year that I entered first grade, seventeen southern and Border States legally mandated separate schools for blacks and whites. I was one of the nearly 39 percent of students in the United States who attended segregated schools.

I began my schooling uneventfully in a large, ramshackle building in Jackson County, Florida. There isn't much I remember about those days with the exception of the dirt playground, the sale of one-cent cookies at noon, and getting spanked by my first grade teacher for refusing to say "yes ma'am." I preferred to acknowledge her with a respectful "yes, Mrs. Keith." I suppose the most noteworthy aspect of that year was that due to the complete lack of oversight of black schools, I started school undetected at five years of age.

My second and third grades were spent in Marion, Virginia. I attended a redbrick school funded by seed money from the Rosenwald Fund to construct African American schools; it was built by black craftsmen, on land donated by local black residents. The Carnegie School consisted of four classrooms, an auditorium upstairs, and a cafeteria and girls' bathroom in the basement. Boys had to go outside to enter their restroom, also located in the basement.

Carnegie was typical of many black schools in the South; both elementary and secondary students attended the same school. High school instruction at Carnegie went only to eleventh grade; however, students who finished there were able to matriculate at black colleges in the surrounding states.

There were three teachers and one teacher-principal at Carnegie. Miss Thompson, who became a major influence and role model in my life, taught grades 1, 2, and 3, as well as being the music teacher for the entire school. Mrs. Campbell taught grades, 4, 5, and 6; Miss Ellis taught grades 7, 8, and 9; and Professor Dabney taught the tenth and eleventh grades as well as being the principal. Miss Ellis and Professor Dabney provided the basic courses for junior and high school students at Carnegie without the benefit of a science lab or library. Remarkably, Carnegie boasts of many graduates who went on to attend college and become successful in their careers.

I concluded my elementary schooling at Baker Academy, located in Punta Gorda, Florida. The school board had previously named the school in honor of the first principal; however, it was not felt that the school was worthy of being called a school—thus the name Baker Academy. In this original three-room school, two teachers and one teacher/principal taught grades 1 through 6. Mrs. Smith, the principal, taught the first and second grades; Mrs. Bailey taught the third and fourth grades; and Mrs. Clemons, fifth and sixth grades. Shortly after the *Brown v. Board of Education* decision declared segregated schools unconstitutional, the county added a fourth room, which housed the combination library and cafeteria. Bathrooms were located outside.

As an elementary school student, I never read from a textbook that had not been written in or otherwise marred by the previous owners. I sat in old graffiti-covered desks that were discards from the white schools. Mostly, I depended upon the largesse of my teachers to supply the materials and resources that were needed.

I also had, although being quite shy, appeared in numerous plays and programs, learned to "stand and deliver" voluminous poems, and developed a sense of confidence in my ability as a student. I did not know what it meant to have low expectations held of my abilities or doubts about what I would be able to accomplish later in my life.

In 1956, two years after the *Brown* decision, my mother caused the first ripple in our county related to equal educational opportunities for black children. I was slated to go to seventh grade the next fall, and the all-black school that I attended went only to sixth grade. There was a white high school in town, but black students were bused past the white high school to attend Dunbar High School, a black school twenty-five miles away; this meant a fifty-mile-a-day round-trip. Students left at 7:00 in the morning and returned at 5:30 in the afternoon. Those who wished to participate in extracurricular activities had to find their own transportation home or stay overnight with friends or family in the area.

My mother, who like her aunts before her had to live away from home to receive a secondary education, was vehemently opposed to my having to be bused fifty miles a day. She tested the waters. My mother went to the school board and made a simple request for my transportation costs and living expenses so that I could live with my aunt and attend school in another county. The school board predictably refused, saying that if they did it for one they would have to do it for all parents who did not want their children bused. Probably fearing further action on my mother's part, the school board hastily placed two portable classrooms to accommodate the seventh and eighth grades at the all-black school in our town.

I did not attend school in those portables and went on to attend Booker High School in a nearby county. This arrangement would allow me to have a normal high school experience while being able to come home on weekends. Booker High School was actually a new, state-of-the-art facility (by black school standards) when I entered seventh grade. As was the case in many school districts in the South, the construction of new, modern facilities was meant as an enticement to keep black students attending predominately black segregated schools.

The *Brown* decision was to have no bearing on my elementary or secondary education. When I graduated from segregated Booker High School in Sarasota, Florida, in 1962, most schools in the South were still segregated. The white high school in my hometown was voluntarily desegregated two years after I graduated from high school.

When I graduated from Booker High School, I was a shy but academically confident student who applied to and was accepted into a predominately white university in the Midwest. Although this was my first integrated school experience, I graduated with a solid "B" average and without missing a beat. I did not need developmental or remedial courses (I am not even sure they existed then). My only "lack" was year two of Spanish.

At Booker, I had followed a college preparatory course that included Algebra I and II, Geometry, Trigonometry, Biology, Chemistry, and Physics. I had won countywide essay contests and was involved in an array of extracurricular activities that offered me the opportunity to develop self-presentation and leadership skills.

In spite of the lack of resources that my schools faced, I do not believe that I received an "inferior" education. I graduated high school confident in my abilities and, despite the racial oppression that was pervasive in the early 1960s, I believed without a doubt that my education would make a difference in my life. Most of all, I understood that getting an education served a larger purpose.

I graduated from my racially segregated high school almost fifty years ago. Over those years, through my roles as parent and educator, I have watched and waited for the educational equality that was promised to children like me to become a reality. I find that my segregated schooling experiences are in stark contrast to those of southern black and brown children attending segregated schools today. We have come full circle. We have gone from the historically segregated black schools that I attended in the South through a tumultuous period of resistance, including forced desegregation, only to end with a return to segregation—a very different kind of segregation and one much more onerous than that which I experienced.

Acknowledgments

A very special thanks to the following:

Dr. Tom Koerner, for his interest in this topic and his willingness to trust me to develop the concept into a book.

Lindsey Schauer, for her guidance and thoughtful feedback on the manuscript.

Dr. Teresa Hill, for her review of the manuscript and very helpful comments.

Anitta Orr, for her detailed and thoughtful critique of the manuscript.

Richard Carey, for his very skillful technical assistance.

Jaha, my son, for reminding me that with awareness comes responsibility and of my obligation "to tell the truth," as he put it, about the school experiences of poor minority children.

Saba, my daughter, who kept me abreast of the most recent developments in educational policy and insisted that the ideas presented in this book be relevant to the current conversation about school reform.

David, my companion, for his continued encouragement, support, and nutritious meals.

The parents and students who, for the last twenty years, have allowed me to hear and know their stories.

Introduction

In 1954, in *Brown v. Board of Education*, the U.S. Supreme Court outlawed racially segregated schools, stating that they (black schools) were "inherently inferior." While there was some trepidation among African Americans because of their experiences in dealing with white attitudes in the South, by and large they saw the *Brown* decision as a symbol of hope. However, the euphoria they felt was short-lived. It would be ten years before any noticeable movement in the direction of school desegregation occurred. When desegregation through massive busing did finally begin, it came with great sacrifice to African Americans; black schools were closed and black teachers fired or demoted.

The wave of desegregation did bring significant gains for many black students. From 1964 to the late 1980s, the black–white achievement gap closed substantially, particularly in the South (Orfield, 2005). At the same time, black high school graduation and college attendance rates were increasing. Access to greater opportunities in higher education and subsequently the job market was the most significant gain for black students deemed "exceptions." Both of my own children attended Ivy League colleges as a result of desegregation; recruiters from these schools routinely recruited from high schools like the one they attended.

The vision of equal educational opportunity that African Americans had in mind and sought for their children, however, was not to be fully realized. At the time of the *Brown* decision, African Americans rationalized that if their children were attending the same schools and sitting in the same classrooms, they could not help but receive the same education. As one minister remarked, "If we are all riding in the same air conditioned car, I will be as cool as the person sitting next to me." Just as that analogy is

1

flawed, the mechanism for bringing about educational equity through the desegregation process proved to be flawed as well.

For the masses of black children, desegregation meant being bused to schools where they sensed they did not belong and in many instances experienced outright hostility from students and even teachers. They were isolated in low-level and special education classes and were not highly represented in extracurricular activities except for athletics.

While the 1954 *Brown* decision opened the door for laws that would change the racial landscape of the United States, some fifty years later, the masses of children from what Ogbu (1978) terms "caste minorities" still languish in schools that fail to adequately educate them. The deeply rooted problems that plagued pre-*Brown* segregated schools persist, and a new set of problems inherent in the "new" segregation have emerged.

A post-*Brown* segregation has evolved which, in many ways, is far more insidious than that experienced by blacks of previous generations. The "new" post-*Brown* segregation has created a class of "chronically undereducated students"; these, as a result, perpetuate to a large extent the "underclass" in this nation.

The post-*Brown* segregated schools are populated in most instances by poor rural and urban minority students who attempt to learn under a cloud of inferiority as they and their schools are labeled "low-performing." They are taught by the least prepared teachers in terms of both attitudes and skills, and, as in pre-*Brown* segregation, they most often attend dilapidated, overcrowded, underfunded schools. These students struggle to be inspired by less than stimulating, repetitive lessons to prepare them for tests that will once more give witness to their intellectual inferiority.

Because we live under the illusion that we are a "postracial" and "classless" society, the schooling of these children will provide no mechanism for them to address the most pressing and crucial issues that impact their life conditions. In the end, these angry, frustrated students' sense of powerlessness explodes as they act out or simply refuse to attend our schools. These chronically undereducated students will leave our schools and replicate the choices of their parents and grandparents. Another generation will be trapped in the underclass by the new segregation.

There are many books that address the resegregation of our nation's schools and the inequities that continue to characterize schools attended primarily by students from caste minority groups, especially those in urban areas. The purpose of this book is to describe the character and effects of post-*Brown* segregation, especially in schools in the deep South. In particular, a basic "marker" of pre-*Brown* segregated schools, the *ideology of inferiority*, is examined. This ideology, which justified segregation in all aspects of southern life, was used to maintain the unequal social standing of blacks.

It is posited that the degree to which the ideology of inferiority informs the structure and context of the educational process for poor minority students is indicative of the extent to which these students will fail to experience equal educational opportunities. It is suggested that as long as this ideology undergirds the policies and practices of schools attended by these students, their educational outcomes will remain dismal.

This book explores the impact of the post-*Brown* segregation upon the achievement and aspirations of students from caste minority groups. In doing so, the differences in two major areas—school culture and school climate—are examined in the pre- and post-*Brown* segregated schools. In addition, given the reality of a return to segregated schools in this nation, steps are suggested that must be taken to ensure equal educational opportunities for children from caste minority groups in the "new" segregated schools.

As the government plans to implement a four-billion-dollar Race to the Top stimulus plan to encourage rigorous standards, improve student performance, and especially to improve teacher quality in schools serving poor students, the critical issues and problems resulting from post-*Brown* segregation must be addressed. Any proposed solutions to the problems of schools attended by poor students from caste minority backgrounds must:

- Acknowledge the caste system that exists in the United States and the ways in which one's caste position determines the quality of education that one receives
- Demonstrate the *will*—based upon our acknowledgement of their schooling reality and experiences—to make structural changes in the type of education that chronically undereducated students receive
- Implement a *socially responsive pedagogy* that will provide direct intervention to help chronically undereducated students overcome the obstacles imposed by poverty and caste minority membership

The daily and lived experiences of students who attend post-*Brown* segregated schools have not been examined. It is crucial that we examine and give credence to the actual experience of students as we design reform strategies. We must finally ask what *school-related* factors serve as barriers to achievement among these students and what role *stigmatizing school environments* play in the disengagement and failure of students from caste minority groups. We cannot plan or implement meaningful reform in schools for these students until we answer the following critical questions:

- What are the experiences of caste minority students in low-performing or failing schools?
- What are the beliefs and attitudes of those who teach in and administer schools attended primarily by students from caste minority groups?

- How do these beliefs and attitudes inform the policies and practices that impact the everyday experiences of these students?
- How do the actual school experiences impact the performance and persistence of students from caste minority groups?
- What is the most effective and empowering pedagogy for students from caste minority groups?

If we truly desire to ensure that chronically undereducated students in this nation have equal opportunity to access a quality education that will give them the tools to transcend their underclass condition, we must make some drastic changes in the way in which we think about and structure schooling for these children.

The anecdotal material included in this book comes primarily from my experiences in conducting workshops and providing technical assistance to predominately black low-performing schools in the deep South from the 1990s to 2010. For this reason, this book focuses on the experiences of black children in post-*Brown* segregated schools in the South. However, the term "poor minority children" is used throughout the book, indicating the recognition that students from other minority groups, especially Latino students, are equally segregated and that they in all likelihood have educational experiences similar to those of African American students.

It is important to continue to document the experiences of black children in southern schools because:

- It was on the behalf of black children that *Brown* was inspired.
- The South had the greatest number of blacks, the most comprehensive system of racial subordination, and the deepest resistance to social change (Orfield, 2005).
- Southern schools became the most desegregated but now show a trend toward greater segregation (Orfield, 2005).
- The newly resegregated schools are often those that are designated as low-performing schools by the No Child Left Behind (NCLB) Act of 2001.
- Black children continue to be the primary focus of analysis related to poor educational outcomes.

Part I of this book addresses the problems posed by the new post-*Brown* segregation. The first chapter provides an overview of the evolution of post-*Brown* segregated schools. In chapter 2, pre- and post-*Brown* segregation are contrasted and the new segregation is examined.

In part II, factors influencing the daily experience of students in low-performing post-*Brown* segregated schools are explored. In chapter 3, the culture of low-performing post-*Brown* segregated schools is described, and Chapter 4 focuses on the climate or *stigmatizing environments* characteristic of many low-performing segregated schools. Chapter 5 is devoted to the impact of the culture and climate upon the academic identity, esteem, and achievement of students attending low-performing segregated schools.

In part III, the needs of chronically undereducated students are examined and strategies for reforming the schools they attend are discussed. In chapter 6, the ways in which the pre-*Brown*, historically black segregated schools helped students to transcend the racial stigma imposed by Jim Crow are discussed. Chapter 7, focuses on the reality of effectively educating students in post-*Brown* segregated schools and outlines the four aspects of *socially responsive pedagogy*. Finally, chapter 8 provides a discussion of *will* and our commitment to educating all students in this society.

James Anderson (1988), the noted historian, suggested that the struggles carried out by black people for education in this country could be thought of as "crusades." The first crusade occurred when ex-slaves waged a campaign to establish free public education in the South; the second crusade involved the expansion of black segregated schools. The movement to desegregate our nation's schools in an effort to achieve equal educational opportunity for all students can be thought of as the third crusade.

As we enter the twenty-first century, circumstances insist that we engage in a new crusade, a fourth crusade if you will, to restore the promise of *Brown*. This crusade must be one of honesty and realism, one that addresses the real issues and finally removes the obstacles to equal educational opportunity. The fourth crusade must be a demonstration of our will to finally live up to our democratic principles and ensure that our schools, commensurate with their noble purpose, are vehicles for improving life chances and making the American dream accessible to all children.

This book is intended as a guide to starting a "real" discussion about the education of poor minority children in this country. The resegregation of schools coupled with the "color-blind ideology" signals a return to an old way of thinking that then and now denies equal educational opportunity to all of the nation's children. We must acknowledge that, since *Brown*, we have come full circle—that we again have a dual school system in this nation, and that children in the new post-*Brown* schools are chronically undereducated.

The ideas expressed in this book will certainly not be embraced by all. It is hoped, however, that administrators and teachers who work in schools (charter schools included) that are low-performing or failing and who are frustrated with ineffective and punitive reform strategies will see the ideas expressed herein as an alternative approach to improving educational outcomes for the students they teach.

If we can be honest with ourselves, if we have the desire to create and live in a fully equal and free society, we can transform our schools into institutions that educate and empower rather than further perpetuate the underclass. *Brown* was a decision based primarily upon legal principles, the denial of rights guaranteed under the Fourteenth Amendment; now it is time to make a clearly moral decision about the education of poor minority children in this nation.

It is time to decide if we as a nation have the will to reform our schools so that they truly reflect our creed as a democratic society. The choice we make will affect our very future as a nation.

Part I

BROWN'S UNKEPT PROMISE

1

The Road from Segregation to Resegregation

The 1954 U.S. Supreme Court *Brown v. Board of Education* decision declaring segregation in public schools unconstitutional was regarded as one of the great milestones in U.S. history and for blacks a pronouncement second in importance only to the Emancipation Proclamation, which had ended slavery almost a century before (Muse, 1964). However, within ten years of actual compliance through massive busing, the tide began to turn and the return to legalized segregation in schools began. By the fiftieth anniversary of the monumental *Brown* decision, the backward slide toward resegregation of public schools had already begun (Orfield, 2005).

As we enter the twenty-first century, we face a new form of racial segregation in schools that in many ways is more deleterious than that which was the impetus for *Brown*. Despite the hopes of African Americans, a return to segregation was a foreseeable ending to a process fraught with resistance, the total destruction of "black education," and the unfair burden imposed on black children and communities.

In this chapter, the evolutionary process of the return to legally segregated schools is examined. The progression to resegregated schools occurred in three overlapping phases, all with the intention of maintaining the status quo and perpetuating the racial caste system (table 1.1). The first phase, *resistance*, which began immediately after *Brown* and continues even today, involved both overt and covert resistance. In the *pragmatic* phase, the greatest wave of desegregation occurred; at this same time however, a *redesign of segregation*, allowing segregation within desegregated settings, was fashioned. Finally, in the third phase, *dismantling*, legal decisions, a return to neighborhood schools, and the advent of *color-blind education* completed the process of the return to legally segregated schools. As shown later in this

9

Table 1.1.　The Evolution of Resegregation in Public Schools

1896–1954 Legal Segregation	1954–1964 Resistance to Desegregation	1964–1974 Pragmatic Desegregation	1974–1995 Dismantling Desegregation	2000 Resegregation
Plessey v. Ferguson decision, 1896	Overt resistance	1964 Civil Rights Act/1965 Elementary and Secondary Education Act (ESEA)	U.S. Supreme Court decisions	Segregated neighborhood schools
	White flight		Overt/covert resistance	Color-blind education
	Massive resistance		Unitary status	
		Massive busing		
		Overt/covert resistance		
		Segregation within desegregated settings		

chapter, the ideology that rationalized the segregation of schools remained firmly intact and the status quo was preserved.

THE DECISION

> We conclude that in the field of public education the doctrine of separate but equal has no place. Separate educational facilities are inherently unequal.
>
> —*Brown v. Board of Education*, 1954

The Court ruled that state-imposed segregation was inherently discriminatory and was therefore a denial of the equal protection clause of the Fourteenth Amendment. The ruling established that black children attending school in segregated districts were deprived of the equal protection of the laws guaranteed by the Fourteenth Amendment.

The NAACP's line of argument was the "inequality of separateness" and relied upon the testimony of psychologists and sociologists stating that segregation had detrimental personality effects upon Negro children and impaired their ability to profit from available facilities of public education (Muse, 1964). The results of the doll studies conducted by Kenneth and

Mamie Clark, in particular, were used to maintain that segregation accentuated feelings of inferiority among Negro children (Patterson, 2001).

However, the unanimous eleven-page opinion, read by Chief Justice Earl Warren, was written in such a way as not to further antagonize the South and to give the South "time to cope" (Patterson, 2001). Another hearing would allow attorneys general throughout the South to identify the best ways of implementing the decision. According to Muse (1964), the "great decision" accomplished no immediate and sweeping transformations, as it was not obeyed in all sections of the South for many years to come.

BROWN II

The second opinion, *Brown II*, issued a year later on May 31, 1955, contained the ambivalent and highly criticized phrase "with all deliberate speed" as well as other equivocal language. The ruling did not call upon the lower federal courts to require that school districts submit desegregation plans within any particular time period, and it did not set any fixed date for the end of segregated schools (Patterson, 2001).

The South reacted to *Brown II* with a feeling of relief, as it was taken as permission to proceed slowly. This interpretation was bolstered by a U.S. district court decision in the South Carolina *Briggs v. Elliot* case (Clotfelter, 2004). The 1955 *Briggs v. Elliot* ruling threatened to dilute the strength of *Brown*, as it ruled that the Constitution does not require integration; it merely forbids the use of governmental power to enforce segregation. As a result of the *Briggs v. Elliot* ruling, southern officials began to adopt a range of ruses to avoid the appearance of using racial considerations as the basis of assigning students to schools (Patterson, 2001).

PHASE I: RESISTANCE

African Americans generally believed and expected that the *Brown* decision would bring about immediate change. Even Thurgood Marshall was optimistic, estimating that segregated schools could be eliminated in the nation within five years (Patterson, 2001). The mood in the South was predictably and decidedly different. The immediate reaction of the South was that the *Brown* decision was an instrument to destroy "a central pillar of its social order" (Clotfelter, 2004).

The resistance to Brown began immediately and was initially expressed overtly by political leaders, public officials, parents, and demagogues. For purposes of this discussion, "overt resistance" refers to those actions that clearly expressed an aversion to racial mixing as the reason for dissent.

Overt resistance was expressed in several forms: political actions to thwart *Brown*, militant resistance (i.e., those acts that incited or called for mob or individual acts of violence), and white flight.

"Covert resistance" in this discussion refers to actions taken that seemingly express personal preference or other reasons unrelated to race per se. Primarily, it refers to those actions taken at the school level, ostensibly based upon educational policy, that maintained segregation. While this first phase of the progression to resegregation is termed resistance, resistance of some order occurred at every phase of the desegregation process.

POLITICAL RESISTANCE

The reaction of southern leaders was totally one of defiance; they aggressively resisted the *Brown* decision in all respects. According to Orfield (2005), there was intense state and local resistance from virtually all white leaders as the entire elected leadership of the region mobilized under the banner of "massive resistance." Congressmen from the region denounced the decision in a sectional statement of resistance known as the Southern Manifesto. This statement accused the Supreme Court of abuse of judicial power and promised to use all legal means to reverse the decision (Patterson, 2001; Clotfelter, 2004).

The most effective political resistance was expressed at the state level in terms of laws and constitutional amendments aimed at evading compliance with Brown (Bartley, 1997; Patterson, 2001). Southern governors, state legislatures, and local officials began in earnest to devise plans to evade the decision and to stimulate popular support for resistance (Muse, 1964). For example, Georgia made it a felony for any state or local official to spend public funds on desegregated schools; Mississippi and Louisiana declared it illegal for children to attend racially mixed schools; South Carolina denied state funds to schools complying with desegregation orders; and Virginia pioneered the strategy of " massive resistance" (Bartley, 1997; Patterson, 2001).

The resistance to *Brown I* and *II* took the form of delaying, rebuffing, and frustrating the efforts of blacks to desegregate schools as well as the use of economic leverage, intimidation, and other forms of social control (Cecelski, 1994). An initial strategy used by many districts, including the one in which I attended school, was to improve black schools. Efforts were immediately undertaken to greatly reduce the disparities in black and white schools in the hope that black students would remain in their schools and black parents would be dissuaded from taking legal action. As a result, new schools were built and facilities upgraded.

A tactic adopted by southern districts was to institute a policy of "freedom of choice," which permitted parents to send children to the schools of their choice. This voluntary desegregation was designed to strategically allow a small number of black students to enroll in white schools in order to reduce vulnerability to lawsuits. The procedures, however, were complicated, the criteria were vague, and of course the intended result was the denial of transfer to black students.

Another strategy involved placing power into the hands of local citizens to make the decision to desegregate or not. For instance, the Pearsall Plan, devised in North Carolina, gave local citizens the power to close schools by popular referendum if desegregation occurred and permitted state tuition to go to white students attending private schools in these districts.

The most popular and widely adopted strategies, which allowed local school officials to legally avoid desegregation under state law, were the Pupil Assignment Laws. These laws stipulated that local districts could assign students to schools on the basis of complicated psychological and academic criteria (i.e., aptitude, conduct, morals, health, and the personal standards of the pupil). The goal, of course, was to perpetuate segregated schools (Patterson, 2001). In North Carolina, the Pearsall Plan and the Pupil Assignment Act enabled local school districts to avoid desegregation for more than a decade (Cecelski, 1994).

MILITANT RESISTANCE

Militant resistance to desegregation that appealed to intimidation and violence took many forms. Intimidation and social control were used to prevent black parents from sending their children to white schools. Economic coercion was used against blacks who were vulnerable to employers, landlords, and creditors. Emotional appeals to the "cause of the Confederacy," alarms of social and sexual mingling, and the specter of communism were commonplace (Patterson, 2001).

After the *Brown* rulings, "diehard anti-Negro" sentiment solidified in the South; states' rights and anti–Supreme Court zealots arose; the Ku Klux Klan gained strength; white Citizens' Councils proliferated; and violence against blacks increased (Muse, 1964; Patterson, 2001). Token desegregation—which occurred in places like Clinton and Nashville, Tennessee; Charlotte, North Carolina; New Orleans, Louisiana; and Little Rock, Arkansas—was accompanied by mob violence. Resistance to school desegregation was such that by early 1964, only about 1 percent of black children in the eleven southern states attended schools with whites (Patterson, 2001).

WHITE FLIGHT

A major form of resistance to desegregation, which began during the early stages and persists today, is white flight. Either through enrollment in private schools or movement into segregated residential neighborhoods, whites have managed to avoid attendance in schools with any or many minority students.

According to Clotfelter (2004), soon after the *Brown* decision, private schools became a vehicle of escape from desegregation. In Prince Edward County, Virginia, when officials closed public schools rather than desegregate them, whites organized private schools through support from public and nonprofit funds. All-white segregation academies sprang up in Mississippi and other states in the region in the late 1960s.

Massive busing to achieve desegregation during the pragmatic phase brought great overt and covert resistance from whites; in many urban districts, white flight undid efforts to desegregate the schools. According to Clotfelter (2004), declining white enrollment was common in many large, desegregated school districts during the period of large-scale desegregation orders. While the expressed reason for residential choices may have related to the desire for "better or good schools," research shows that "other things being equal, whites prefer schools and classrooms that are all-white or predominately white" and that, especially when nonwhite percentages in schools were higher, whites took measures to avoid these schools (Clotfelter, 2004).

Finally, segregation within segregated settings or "a school within a school" is a strategy employed to maintain segregated classrooms. In the immediate aftermath of desegregation efforts in the 1960s, some southern districts established classrooms that were completely segregated by race. A much more common strategy used to maintain segregated classrooms is ability grouping and tracking.

Epstein (1985) found that ability grouping within classes was more often used in the South by teachers who had negative views of the educational benefits of desegregation and in classrooms with more blacks. According to Meier (1989), academic grouping and discipline are two means by which interracial contact can be limited in desegregated school settings. Black students were generally less likely to be assigned to advanced or honors classes and more likely to be assigned to special education tracks for the mentally retarded. Discipline practices in the form of unwarranted or excessive suspensions ultimately maintained segregation by removing black students from the school setting.

Within-school segregation persists in desegregated schools. Clotfelter (2004) found that patterns of within-school segregation tended to be highest in schools with larger percentages of black students and to be higher in middle and high schools than in elementary schools. As late as 2002, in school districts in which I worked, examples of within-school segregation—including separate seating (i.e., "death rows," made up of all black boys), separate all-white social clubs and student organizations, as well as the usual tracking—were found in schools seeking a "unitary status" designation, indicating that the school district had eliminated the old racially segregated dual school system.

PHASE II: PRAGMATIC DESEGREGATION

While the *Brown* decision undermined the legitimacy of Jim Crow, it mandated almost no change. Almost a decade after *Brown I* and *II*, 99 percent of all black students were still attending totally segregated schools (Orfield, cited in Anderson & Byrne, 2004). It would take the Civil Rights Act of 1964 and the Elementary and Secondary Education Act (ESEA) to breathe new life into the desegregation process, prompting a *pragmatic* form of desegregation.

Pragmatic desegregation for purposes of this discussion is defined as a form of desegregation that maintained traditional patterns of white privilege and power over education while ostensibly abiding by the Supreme Court decision and reaping needed financial benefits for local school districts. Desegregation that occurred as a result of massive busing is included in pragmatic desegregation because white privilege and power prevailed while black children bore the brunt of the burden of busing.

According to Orfield (2005), widespread desegregation was achieved in the South with the passage of the 1964 Civil Rights Act. President Johnson, who was committed to enforcing the law, brought the power of the federal government to bear on southern school districts. Title IV of the law authorized the U.S. Department of Justice to initiate class action lawsuits against recalcitrant school districts and Title VI allowed the withholding of funds from any districts that excluded students from school on the basis of race (Clotfelter, 2004).

The 1964 Civil Rights Act and the Elementary and Secondary Education Act, passed in 1965, which provided federal funding for school districts, especially those in the South, used federal authority, sanctions, and financial incentives to motivate school districts in the South to comply with desegregation orders (Clotfelter, 1999; Orfield, cited in Anderson & Byrne, 2009).

TEN YEARS OF PROGRESS

For approximately ten years, 1964–1974, the combination of presidential commitment, federal authority, and a series of Supreme Court decisions served as an impetus for the desegregation movement in the South. In 1968, in the *Green v. County School Board of New Kent County* decision, the Court struck down freedom-of-choice plans, established for the first time an "affirmative duty" to desegregate, and defined desegregation as the abolition of identifiably white and black schools (Clotfelter, 2004).

Green v. County School Board of New Kent County outlined a set of specific standards that districts had to meet in their efforts to eliminate a segregated school system. Districts that removed the vestiges of segregation (known as the *Green factors*) throughout the specified aspects of school operation (i.e., staff/faculty assignments, transportation, facilities, and extracurricular activities) would be considered to have converted from a dual to a *unitary* system (Smrekar & Goldring, 2009). The 1969 *Alexander and Holmes* decision unanimously ordered that schools be desegregated "at once" (Clotfelter, 2004).

Massive busing became the means to accelerate the desegregation of schools with the 1971 *Swann v. Charlotte Mecklenberg Board of Education* decision. This decision ruled that districts could implement crosstown busing and student reassignment strategies to ameliorate the combined effects of segregated housing patterns and the de facto segregation of neighborhood school attendance zones (Smrekar & Goldring, 2009). This ruling made it possible for previously segregated districts to balance their schools racially to the extent possible, even if that required crosstown busing.

These decisions changed the racial landscape of southern schools. By 1970, in terms of schools, the South was the nation's most integrated region (Orfield, cited in Anderson & Byrne, 2009). Some 78 percent of black students had attended schools that were 90 percent or more minority in 1968; by 1972, only 25 percent of black students attended such schools (Clotfelter, 2004).

PHASE III: THE DISMANTLING OF DESEGREGATION AND A RETURN TO SEGREGATION

According to Clotfelter (2004), the turning point in the federal government's stance on the policy of school desegregation began in 1974, when the Supreme Court issued the first in a series of decisions that would effectively slow government efforts to desegregate schools. During the *dismantling* phase of desegregation, the Supreme Court began to set limits, making it more difficult and often impossible to address the remaining problems of segregation and inequity in the metropolitan areas—problems that were based upon segregation among separate school districts (Orfield, 2005).

Milliken v. Bradley marked the beginning of a retreat from proactive pursuit of racial balance as a judicial objective. This decision mandated that federal court orders could not be used to assign students to schools across district lines for the purpose of desegregation; in effect, it said that no desegregation remedy could be extended beyond a single school district. This ruling would therefore prevent the desegregation of metropolitan school districts (Clotfelter, 2004).

It was in the 1990s, however, that the full assault upon desegregation began. Three decisions outlined procedures for court approval of the dismantling of school desegregation plans (Lomack, 2004). According to Orfield (2005), the resegregation of public schools in the South was clearly related to the 1991 *Board of Education of Oklahoma City v. Dowell* decision, which adopted two basic ideas: (1) that desegregation was a temporary rather than a permanent goal for schools and (2) that courts could dissolve existing orders and permit the restoration of segregated neighborhood schools as long as the districts stated that the changes were for educational rather than racial reasons.

Under *Dowell*, a district that briefly took the steps outlined in *Green* and was termed "unitary" could be freed from its legal obligation to purge itself of segregation. The 1992 *Freeman v. Pitts* ruling held that the various requirements laid out in *Green* need not be present at the same time, meaning that a segregated system could dismantle its desegregation plan without fully having met all of the requirements outlined previously in *Green*. The *Dowell* and *Pitts* decisions essentially allowed southern school districts to return to the "natural" pattern of segregation after "the sentence of desegregation" had been served (Orfield & Eaton, 1996).

The 1995 *Missouri v. Jenkins* ruling prohibited efforts to attract white suburban and private school students voluntarily into city schools. The Court ruled that school districts need not show any actual correction of the educational harms of segregation and defined rapid restoration of local control as the primary goal in desegregation cases (Orfield & Eaton, 1996).

These three rulings brought a flurry of activity from southern school districts eager to be removed from Court oversight. These rulings also opened the way for black students to be sent back to segregated neighborhood schools. By 2001 and the introduction of the No Child Left Behind law, the return to segregated schools in the South was complete. As southern school officials won full control of school districts, "separate and unequal" again became the norm.

While a number of factors—such as increasing numbers of minority students, especially Latinos; the decline in numbers of white students in the South's public schools; and the spread of housing segregation—all contributed to the return to segregated schools in the South, Orfield (2005) suggests that the resegregation of these public schools has clearly been related to court decisions. Equally important, all three branches of the federal government supported limiting civil rights enforcement, and a return to racial subordination and inequality has become acceptable (Boger & Orfield, 2005).

THE IDEOLOGY OF INFERIORITY

After only a decade of aggressive movement toward the desegregation of the nation's schools and the promise of equal educational opportunity for all students, the resegregation of public schools was imminent. What actions taken or not taken contributed to this reversal and why did the nation so readily accept the return to a segregated public school system?

First and foremost, not once at the initiation of the desegregation process or during it was the basis for segregation, the ideology of racial and cultural inferiority, refuted. Second, throughout the process, the actions taken by school officials responsible for implementing desegregation expressed a belief in the ideology of inferiority. Finally, as a result of the actions or inaction of national, regional, and local leaders, no real change occurred in the national consciousness with regard to the beliefs rooted in the ideology.

Rather than desegregation being viewed as an affirmation of our democratic principles and in the national interest, it was viewed as a burden, a loss of privilege, and a giving in to the whims of undeserving inferiors. The ideology of racial and cultural inferiority is ingrained in the consciousness of the nation. It is, in fact, this consciousness or belief in the inferiority of minorities (i.e., African Americans, Mexican Americans, Native Americans, etc.) that sets them apart and assigns them to a low-caste position in the society (Ogbu, 1978).

Because of the legacy of slavery, however, this ideology is most strongly and persistently attached to blacks. It was the ideology of racial and cultural inferiority that was used to rationalize slavery, to justify discrimination, and to establish and maintain separate and unequal schools for blacks.

THE LACK OF PERSUASIVE AUTHORITY

The ideology of black inferiority was firmly planted in the national consciousness first through the writings of Thomas Jefferson, our national hero and authority figure. Jefferson's message became central to the belief system regarding blacks in this society. Scientists, social scientists, historians, and religious leaders who endeavored to create a racist ideology supported by scientific, historical, and religious authority expanded upon the ideology, further entrenching it in the national consciousness.

Persuasive authority had given credence and power to the ideology. A weakening of such an entrenched national belief system required the voice of another national hero to help the nation understand the basis of segregation and the moral imperative of desegregation as an affirmation and application of the nation's democratic creed. Unfortunately, this was not to come about.

President Eisenhower, at the time of the *Brown* decision, enjoyed enormous public standing and popularity; he was also admired by influential whites in the South. It was felt that if Eisenhower spoke out strongly for the decision that others, including obstructionists, would listen (Patterson, 2001). Unfortunately, Eisenhower took no action to endorse the desegregation decision at any time during his presidency, made little effort to inspire compliance with the decision, and was reluctant to send federal troops when desegregation orders (as at Little Rock) met with violent resistance (Bartley, 1997; Clotfelter, 1996; Patterson, 2001).

THE IDEOLOGY OF INFERIORITY PERSISTS

The ideology of inferiority influenced and controlled the process of desegregation in the South. The very same officials who had maintained segregated schools and vehemently opposed desegregation were responsible for devising and implementing desegregation plans. Because the ideology of inferiority remained unchallenged, the creation of equitable education for all children was neither the motivation nor the goal. According to Cecelski (1994), after waging prolonged and unsuccessful struggles to resist desegregation, southern officials rechanneled their energies and influence toward controlling the meaning and nature of desegregation. They designed desegregation plans that preserved the traditional pattern of white privilege and power.

With the ideology of black intellectual and cultural inferiority as its justification, historical black education was destroyed. The early stages of desegregation resulted in the mass closing of black schools rather than a reconciliation of black and white schools on an equal basis. Cecelski (1994) suggests that between 1965 and 1968, the closings of black schools and attempts to efface their legacy became a standard part of school desegregation.

The wholesale closing of black schools meant the firing of black teachers, the elimination and demotion of black principals, the loss of athletic coaches and guidance counselors, all of whom were deemed by the ideology of inferiority to be poorly trained and ineffectual. The most profound effect, and one that continues to serve as a barrier to the participation of

---

Textbox 1.1. Beliefs Expressed about African American Teachers in 2002

- They are not well trained.
- They attended historically black colleges and universities (HBCUs).
- They are not as intelligent.
- They are not as creative and resourceful as whites.
- African American teachers make good coaches, not good teachers.
- They are tokens because of the need for profile.
- They are not capable of teaching higher-level courses.
- They expect leniency.
- They do not follow through on expectations.
- They do not adhere to school rules (e.g., chewing gum, wearing hats, perpetually late).
- They are more strict and stern.
- They had high esteem in segregated schools, but this is not the case in integrated schools.

---

black parents in their children's education was the loss of power felt by black parents and communities.

Beliefs about the inferiority of black teachers is so entrenched that fifty years after *Brown*, the same beliefs continue to be expressed and serve as barriers to the hiring of minority teachers in an urban southern school district seeking to be declared unitary. As part of the consent decrees, school districts seeking unitary status were required to increase the numbers of minority faculty in the district. Textbox 1.1 lists beliefs held about African American teachers in one such southern school district. The paucity of African American teachers, in the South at least, may in part be due to beliefs held about their efficacy that are rooted in the ideology of inferiority, which persist.

DESEGREGATION: A ONE-WAY STREET

The persistence of the ideology of inferiority was apparent in the one-sided implementation of desegregation in the South. Once massive busing was utilized as a means to desegregate schools, black children bore the burden. They took early-morning, tiring bus rides long distances to schools where they initially were not welcomed. Even with the advent of multiple and single grade centers (e.g., sixth-grade centers), black children were bused the longest period of years at the greatest distances.

While the implication was that black children could only be properly schooled in white settings, the specter of their supposed inferiority relegated the masses of black children to lower-level classes and special education. While the pragmatic period of desegregation increased the numbers of black children attending school with white children, this can best be characterized as a period of massive busing and pronounced patterns of segregation within ostensibly desegregated settings.

This type of resegregation, which occurred especially in the South and in secondary school settings, undermined the entire concept of desegregation, as it minimized equal-status interaction through interracial contact and denied students exposure to similar educational expectations and experiences (Eyler, Cook, & Ward, 1983).

Ability grouping, tracking, and placement into special education were the primary methods by which the ideology of inferiority was perpetuated. Black students entering newly desegregated schools were disproportionately segregated into lower-level and remedial classes. At the secondary level, they were most like to be placed in vocational or general tracks. Black students were also disproportionately placed into stigmatizing special education programs such as educable mentally retarded (EMR). Finally, beliefs about the character of black students were evidenced in their disproportionate suspensions in schools that had recently undergone desegregation (Eyler, Cook, & Ward, 1983; Meier, Stewart, & England, 1989).

RESEGREGATION OF PUBLIC SCHOOLS

The Third Generation (Network of Regional Desegregation Centers, 1989), a report describing progress in the desegregation of the nation's public schools, was compiled by the directors of the ten Title IV Desegregation Assistance Centers (DACS). The centers, founded under a provision of the Civil Rights Act of 1964, are funded by the federal government to assist schools and communities involved in school desegregation. The report described "first-," "second-," and "third-generation" problems related to the desegregation process.

First-generation problems were those related to the physical desegregation of schools. The persistence of the ideology of inferiority was evident in the report, which indicated that some ten years after desegregation, a "second generation" of problems were evident in attitudes, policies, and practices, even though schools were physically integrated. The day-to-day school experiences and educational outcomes for black students continued to be impacted by low teacher expectations, stereotyping, and cultural insensitivity.

"Third-generation" problems were described as persistent barriers to integration and the attainment of equal educational outcomes for all groups of students. While a reasonable level of physical integration had occurred in southern school districts, there continued to exist differential achievement between black and white students as well as subtle attitudinal and structural elements that limited equal opportunity.

Even as the desegregation process was being dismantled by Supreme Court decisions in the 1990s, subtle attitudes and structures rooted in the ideology of inferiority continued to impact the learning environment and school experiences of minority students. A significant number of complaints were filed against school districts related to racially hostile school environments. African American parents complained of teacher insensitivity, differential disciplinary practices, tracking, and premature labeling of students (e.g., special education). The well-publicized Jena Six case brought to light the racial harassment that black students endured in some desegregated school settings.

THE FALLACY OF UNITARY STATUS

A unitary school district is assumed to be one that no longer operates two separate systems, one black and one white, and that is assumed to have repaired the damage caused by generations of segregation and overt discrimination (Orfield & Eaton, 1996). Once a district is judged to be unitary, minority students no longer have the protection of the courts and districts no longer face a requirement to maintain a desegregated system.

As school districts rushed to seek unitary status, which would make a return to legally segregated schools possible, significant problems remained related to the persistence of the ideology of inferiority. Significant racial achievement gaps remained, low expectations for minority achievement were pervasive, tracking continued, disparate placement of minority students in special education and gifted programs was the norm, racial disparity in discipline was epidemic, and drop-out rates for minority students remained high.

Many districts "rushed to unitary status" without attempting to remedy the serious racial inequities that plagued the system. In one particular district, segregation remained the norm. Black students were routinely assigned to lower-level courses and disproportionately placed in special education. Racially exclusive clubs existed, and black students were excluded from extracurricular activities with the exception of athletics. For instance, the lone black cheerleader was routinely not notified of practices and publicly denigrated and humiliated when she failed to perform efficiently on the field without appropriate practice. While one prom was held, two prom queens were selected; one black and one white.

Black and white teachers who complained of racial inequities were harassed and ultimately fired. The black community complained to the school district, but their grievances were ignored. When the students, parents, and members of the community were interviewed and their grievances filed in a report, the report was met with denials and accusations of bias.

Most significantly, the feelings of the African American community differed greatly from the information provided to the Court by the representative of the Justice Department. Local school districts—like the one being described, which sought to dismantle their desegregation plans—were allied in court not only with powerful state officials but also with U.S. Department of Justice representatives (Orfield & Eaton, 1996). It was obvious that the interests of black children in this district were subordinate to the interests of the district seeking unitary status.

By 2001, when No Child Left Behind became the law of the land, the problems related to desegregation lost significance. A return to neighborhood schools meant a return to legally segregated schools, and the ideology of inferiority remained firmly in place. With the destruction of black education, black parents and communities had lost their power to impact the schooling of their children.

2

The "New" Segregation

> To separate them [black children in grade and high schools] from others
> of similar age and qualifications solely because of their race generates a
> feeling of inferiority as to their status in the community that may affect
> their hearts and minds in a way unlikely ever to be undone.
>
> —Earl Warren, *Brown v. Board of Education*, 1954

Segregation is a structure of exclusion and discrimination, the central purpose of which is subjugation (Packard, 2002). Segregation is a device used
to stigmatize and subordinate. The separated or targeted group is labeled
inferior, and their social, political, and economic mobility is severely re-
stricted. The imposition of racially segregated schools after the crusade of
ex-slaves to establish free public schools in the South was for the sole purpose of limiting the educational opportunities of black children.

Segregated schools delineated the inferior position of the students who
attended them and were a mechanism for reinforcing the institution of
segregation. Segregated schools, most significantly, impressed upon their
students their worth and value to the larger society. When students attend
schools in dilapidated buildings, sit in overcrowded classrooms, or lacked
adequate transportation to school, they are "saturated with the belief that
they aren't good enough, clean enough, or smart enough" (Packard, 2002).

A distinguishing feature of the segregated schooling designed by the
"architects of black education" was a "special kind of education" based
upon the concept of racial difference (Bullock, 1970) and scientific racism.
Watkins (2001) suggests that scientific racism provided the rationale for
shaping black education and that the architects of black education with
few exceptions embraced the general precepts of "scientific racism." It was

felt that naturally inferior blacks must always occupy a socially subservient position in society.

The chief ideologist for this special education was General Samuel Armstrong, founder of Hampton Normal and Agricultural Institute. Armstrong's views were influenced by the typical stereotypes held of blacks. He believed that blacks were mentally sluggish, indolent, lazy, and inferior culturally. Most significantly, he believed that blacks were deficient in character and that the focus of education for blacks should not be book knowledge but character, morality, and socialization.

According to Armstrong, character education and hard work were the keys to educating blacks (Watkins, 2001). Armstrong believed that the purpose of education for blacks was to adjust them to a subordinate position in southern society, and he argued that the primary purpose in educating blacks was the development of proper work habits and moral behavior (Anderson, 1988; Watkins, 2001).

Armstrong believed that the Negro should be trained in a manner consistent with his position in American life and that this should be mainly industrial in nature (Bullock, 1970). By this "industrial education" was primarily meant the development of good habits of work and morality as opposed to learning a particular vocational skill (Spring, 2007).

The architects of black education planned and designed what can be termed a "caste education." Caste education has five core elements:

- An ideology of intellectual inferiority, which rationalizes and justifies the denial of equal educational opportunity
- A method of segregating or isolating children from low-caste groups into underfunded schools
- A restrictive curriculum that prepares students with only a limited repertoire of skills
- An emphasis on control and rehabilitating the moral character of the student versus academic preparation
- A focus on "training" versus educating

Caste education as designed would ensure the maintenance of the inferior status of black students by preventing them from competing with whites in the larger society. Caste education was never intended to provide anything resembling a "separate but equal" education; it was strictly education designed to prepare its recipients for second-class citizenship.

THE NEW SEGREGATION

What exactly is the "new" segregation? How are pre-*Brown* Jim Crow school segregation and the new post-*Brown* segregation similar? How do pre- and post-*Brown* segregation differ? The new segregation is both a manifestation of persistent resistance to desegregation and a redesign of the "separate and unequal" concept in a more acceptable form. According to Orfield and Eaton (1996), this resegregation is the restoration of "a natural pattern" of segregated schools after a temporary sentence of desegregation was served. Essentially, post-*Brown* segregation serves the same purpose as the pre-*Brown* Jim Crow–style of school segregation.

The central aspects of pre-*Brown* segregation remain firmly intact. First, both pre- and post-*Brown* segregated schools were established through Supreme Court decisions. Just as Plessy's "separate but equal" concept became the basis for pre-*Brown* segregated schools, the resegregation of schools was made possible through two major court decisions in the 1990s: *Board of Education of Oklahoma City Public Schools v. Dowell* (1991) and *Freeman v. Pitts* (1992).

Second, Kozol's *Shame of a Nation* (2005) highlighted the educational inequities in segregated urban schools. Kozol found dilapidated buildings, antiquated and broken equipment, and overcrowded classrooms, just as in pre-*Brown* segregated schools,. Essentially, he found that predominately minority segregated schools were inadequate and had inequitable financial support.

Third, students who attend the post-*Brown* segregated schools, like those who attended the pre-*Brown* segregated schools, come from stigmatized groups and are labeled as intellectually and culturally inferior. Finally, students attending post-*Brown* segregated schools are also provided with what is comparable to a "special" or "caste" education, befitting their position and status in the society. The "high stakes" testing to which these students are persistently subjected limits the range of curriculum and quality of instruction they receive. Textbox 2.1 provides a summary of the similarities between pre- and post-*Brown* segregated schools.

Textbox 2.1.   Similarities between pre- and post-*Brown* Segregated Schools

Pre-*Brown*

- Legally segregated by law, *Plessy v. Ferguson* (1896).
- Disparities in facilities, resources, funding formulas.
- Students attending segregated schools come from "stigmatized groups."
- Official curriculum designed to prepare students for low-status/menial jobs and inferior social positions.

Post-*Brown*

- Legally segregated by law, *Dowell* (1991), *Pitts* (1992).
- Disparities in facilities, resources, funding formulas.
- Students attending segregated schools come from "stigmatized groups."
- Official curriculum designed to prepare students for low-status/menial jobs and inferior social positions.

While similarities exist between segregated schools in the pre- and post-*Brown* eras, there are definite differences as well. Pre- and post-*Brown* segregated schools differ in three major ways that impact the educational experiences and outcomes of students. First, because most black schools had little or no oversight, administrators and teachers were able to circumvent the "system" by expanding the curriculum and educational experiences offered their students. It was, in fact, the rebelliousness and activism of African American teachers and administrators that thwarted official efforts to provide only a caste education to African American students.

In black schools, despite the official caste curriculum, "literacy training" took precedence over industrial education. According to Bullock (1967), "in an attempt to keep faith with the industrial education movement, some courses in the manual arts were offered in black schools but they were basically supplemental rather than seen as a focal part of the curriculum." In the high school I attended, two years of Home Economics was required for females and two years of Agriculture for males. However, the core curriculum was college preparatory.

Second, while the culture and climate of pre-*Brown*, historically black, segregated schools was based upon the liberating nature of education and belief in the highest potential of students, the culture and climate of post-*Brown* segregated schools are driven by the ideology of inferiority. A key component of pre-*Brown* segregated schools was the "familial" atmosphere and the nurturing teacher–student relationships. The ideology undergirding post-*Brown* segregated schools negatively influences the quality of the curriculum, instruction, teacher–student relationships, and overall educational experience of students attending these schools.

Finally, pre-*Brown* segregated schools utilized mechanisms that helped black students to overcome the stigmatization imposed by the institution of segregation and to understand the liberating nature of education. In the new post-*Brown* segregated schools, the institutions themselves are stigmatizing elements in the lives of their students. These three core and critical differences make the new post-*Brown* segregation much more deleterious than pre-*Brown* segregation.

STIGMATIZED GROUPS

Fischer and colleagues (1996) describe a caste system as ranking groups economically, politically, and socially. People belong to the ranked groups by virtue of their birth and the privileges of rank are enforced by law and policy. The system is justified by a set of beliefs, about the intellectual and moral superiority of higher-ranked groups (whites in this society) and the intellectual and moral inferiority of lower-ranked members.

In Ogbu's (1987) comparison of minorities in the United States, the major element that most significantly distinguishes "caste minorities" from other minority groups is the stigma of innate inferiority. Ogbu describes groups in this society who have either been enslaved, conquered, or colonized (i.e., African Americans, Native Americans, Mexican Americans, Puerto Rican Americans, Pacific Islanders, and so on) as caste minorities. It is the ideology of inferiority that has provided a rationale and justification for depriving students from caste minority groups an equal education.

It has always been children from caste minority groups who are forced to attend segregated schools. Pre-*Brown* segregation was mandated strictly based upon race. No matter what the income of black families in the South, all blacks—middle class and poor alike—were forced to attend the same schools and subjected to the same educational inequities. In the post-*Brown* era, however, class has become the new arbiter of who attends post-*Brown* segregated schools, and the chronically undereducated who attend the new segregated schools are primarily poor children from caste minority groups.

These students face a triple jeopardy. They are initially stigmatized because they belong to groups perceived to be racially and culturally inferior. Poverty adds a new, even more stigmatizing dimension. In 1959, some 64 percent of black students in the United States lived in poverty, and most of these attended segregated schools in the South (Southern Education Foundation, 2007). Most of these students, however, did not feel particularly stigmatized by their socioeconomic status. Black students from this generation can often be heard to say," We didn't know we were poor; we were just like everybody else." While all blacks labored under the stigma of race, they did not feel the stigma of poverty to as great an extent.

The stigma of poverty today is brutal. Students attending schools populated by other impoverished students are very much aware of their status and powerlessness in this society. Since the 1980s, the morals and values of the poor have been questioned through the use of pejorative labels that stereotype and stigmatize them as a group (Gans, 1995). Now poor students from caste minority groups are not only deemed to be intellectually inferior but also considered to possess other defective character traits resulting from their being brought up in a "culture of poverty." Since the adoption of the "color-blind" ideology (discussed later in detail), stereotypes that were initially attributed to racial groups (i.e., lazy, irresponsible) are now used to denigrate the poor.

Finally, poor minority students suffer the inequality of attending segregated schools that are labeled inferior, that are in themselves stigmatizing, and that do not provide them with a quality education. In addition, Lomack (2004) suggests that norm-referenced testing that attaches sanctions to academic underachievement does a disservice to schools that serve primarily low-income and ethnic minority students, as these schools spend large amounts of time on test preparation to improve test score rankings while sacrificing quality instruction.

A TALE OF TWO SCHOOLS

A 1997 study and description of two neighborhood schools, one black and one white, in a small southern town sheds light on the very different school experiences of black and white students attending post-*Brown* legally segregated schools. Two schools, the names of which have been changed, are described here; they are Mountain Grove, the white school, and City Elementary, the black school.

About the District

Black students made up 85 percent of the school district population. In six of the seven elementary schools, most students were black. School populations ranged from 57 to 97 percent black, with one school having a 100 percent black student body. Only 15 percent of black students attended the predominately white elementary school.

Each of the predominately black schools could be labeled a failing school, as significant disparities existed between the achievement levels of students attending these schools and those attending the predominately white school. Scores for black students lagged behind those of whites at each grade level. White students consistently scored at the 75th percentile or higher and black students' scores averaged at the 33rd percentile.

The Facilities

One of the hallmarks of pre-*Brown* segregated schools was the huge discrepancy in the funding for segregated black and white schools. Black schools were typically older, less well-maintained structures, often without the amenities of auditoriums, gymnasiums, science labs, and even, in some cases, libraries. The condition and appearance of these facilities sent an important message to the students, parents, and community about the value of the students that attended these schools.

Mountain Grove, the virtually all-white neighborhood school, is an older but airy, clean, and very well-maintained facility. The grounds are maintained and the school is painted. It is an inviting environment with murals on the walls representing landscapes and geographic concepts. This is a school environment in which students are obviously valued and the parents have great influence upon school policy and practices.

Across town, the situation is not as cheery. As one arrives at City Elementary, the all-black neighborhood school, one can feel the despair. From all outer appearances, this is a school attended by poor minority students. The structure is old and seriously neglected. Upon entering the building, it is obvious that the facility is in need of a good cleaning and general repair. The most significant sign of neglect, however, is the leaking roof.

The roof at City Elementary has needed repair for quite some time, yet despite requests from the principal, nothing has been done. Typically, on rainy days, three large garbage pails are used to collect water from the leaks. Uncaught water that stands and flows into the hallways is a potential danger to both students and staff.

The rather drab walls, in need of painting, are filled with signs featuring not academic concepts but rather admonitions to stay in line, be quiet, and the ubiquitous exhortations to develop virtues of character (i.e., respect, responsibility, self-discipline). At City Elementary, the focus is obviously on maintaining control rather than academics.

Funding

The budgets for Mountain Grove and City Elementary were comparable for the academic year. In fact City Elementary received $90,000 more than Mountain Grove. The budget for City Elementary was $1,055,049, and the amount allotted to Mountain Grove was $965,956. On paper, this seems to be equitable; both neighborhood schools are receiving nearly equal funding. One might even argue that the black school receives more. However, despite all of the physical problems at City Elementary, only $5,000 in the budget was earmarked for landscape and maintenance.

Curriculum

An expansive and rigorous curriculum provides "curriculum opportunities" and is an indicator of the philosophy of schooling relevant to the student population. What is taught, how it is taught, and to what standards students are held indicates what is believed about the capacity and potential of students. Also, as was the case in pre-*Brown* segregated schools, the official curriculum offered black students was intended to prepare them for low-paying or menial jobs and to maintain their lower social status in the society.

The Department of Education of the state in which the district is located mandated specific time-on-task requirements for the state's course of study. Local school districts were directed to (1) develop time allocations that reflect a balanced school day and (2) provide instructional time of not less than six hours per day. The mandated curriculum for elementary schools in the state included daily instruction in Language Arts, Mathematics, Science,

Social Studies, Physical Education, and sixty minutes weekly of Health, Art, Music, and Computer Education. Interestingly, the state curriculum was compromised at City Elementary.

Major disparities existed between the two schools (as well as with the district's other predominately black schools) with regard to the state-mandated balanced school program for all students. "Curriculum opportunities" did not exist in the post-*Brown* segregated black school. In this case, in keeping with the ideology of "color-blind education" (discussed below), curriculum opportunities were correlated with social class privilege.

Only one elementary school in the district, Mountain Grove, the predominately white school serving middle-class students, came closest to fully implementing a "balanced" curriculum. At Mountain Grove, a Cultural Arts program, which emphasized fine arts and Spanish, was funded by the parent–teacher organization (PTO). It provided $7,776 ($282 per student) to pay the salaries of a music teacher and a Spanish-language teacher, each to provide ten hours of instruction per week.

Poor black students at City Elementary did not have the "curriculum opportunities" afforded students at Mountain Grove. Despite receiving $90,000 more, funds were not budgeted in a way as to provide the same educational opportunities as those received by students at Mountain Grove. The district did not feel that it was appropriate or necessary to fund art and music, although both would have enhanced students' basic reading and mathematics skills. In keeping with the historical concept of caste education and despite *Brown*, these black students were being prepared to assume their assigned roles in the community and to take the menial jobs that awaited them.

While academic support programs provided by state and federal funding were offered at both Mountain Grove and City Elementary, the content and instructional style of the programs differed. The programs offered at Mountain Grove emphasized the integration of skills into the regular academic programs (e.g., journal writing and creative writing), whereas the programs at City Elementary focused on discrete skills (e.g., recognition skills, etc.).

At both Mountain Grove and City Elementary, students had access to computer technology. The inequality was not so much in number of computers but in the quality of instruction related to the use of the technology. Computers at Mountain Grove were utilized for a broader range of activities (e.g., accessing the Internet for research rather than simply for drills to reinforce reading and mathematics skills, as at City Elementary).

City Elementary is not unlike many of the new post-*Brown* segregated neighborhood schools attended by poor minority students. Not only are many of these schools "separate and unequal" in terms of facilities and funding formulas but the true inequality results from the denial of equal educational opportunity as a result of school cultures and climates deeply rooted in the ideology of inferiority. Segregated schools were a primary method of denying equal educational opportunity in the pre-*Brown* era; they serve the same function today.

COLOR-BLIND EDUCATION IN THE POST-*BROWN* ERA

The belief that racism is no longer a major problem in this country and that existing racial inequalities are the product of the culture and character deficiencies of minorities is related to a post–Civil Rights Era ideology. Sociologist Eduardo Bonilla-Silva (2010) terms this ideology "color-blind racism" and argues that this is a new way of expressing prejudicial attitudes. Bonilla-Silva describes color-blind racism as the dominant American racial ideology in the post–Civil Rights Era and says that unlike its predecessor, Jim Crow racism, it is subtle and avoids traditional racist discourse.

One of the hallmarks of post-*Brown* segregation is the illusion that education is now color-blind despite the fact race is the barometer used to measure educational outcomes in this country. It seems as though the legal mandate for the massive busing of children from caste minority groups to white schools had been expected to magically eliminate the core ideology that established segregated schools initially. The ideology that created segregated schools in the pre-*Brown* era is still very much alive and well. All in all, as shown in chapter 1, the old segregation has only been redesigned.

While we profess to be a color-blind society that provides a race-neutral education, it cannot be denied that race continues to be a major arbiter of the quality of education a child receives and that it determines his or her academic success or failure. Race is the norm by which all indicators of academic success or failure are measured (i.e., the black–white achievement gap). While race and racial ideology continue to influence our "educational standards" and decisions regarding educational outcomes, it is disingenuous to claim that education can be or is at this time color-blind.

In this post-*Brown* era of supposedly color-blind education, some critical factors remain the same. The ideology of racial inferiority, stereotypical images, and beliefs continues to inform and shape the education of poor minority students. The illusion of color-blind education is doing irreparable damage to poor children from minority groups. Color-blind education:

- Denies the social reality of the society in which we live
- Denies the continued saliency of race in the educational system
- Denies the reality of the educational experience of children from caste minority groups

- Frees the school from having to deal with the constellation of issues related to race
- Allows the school to accept no responsibility for the failure of children from caste minority groups (i.e., their failure is most often considered the result of character flaws related to poverty)
- Disavows the mass of information related to the relationship between race, poverty, and inequality
- Disavows the research related to teacher expectations and race and culturally relevant pedagogy
- Focuses on symptoms of inequity (e.g., test scores rather than structural issues)
- Denies teachers and administrators the opportunity to confront and change beliefs and attitudes that serve as barriers to the effective education of poor minority children
- Provides no space to confront, challenge, or change the school experience of children who are victims of a stigmatizing school environment
- Allows schools to maintain the status quo and perpetuate the caste system through subtle racial practices

Ultimately, poor minority students are trapped in schools in which they are woefully undereducated—schools that are more damaging in many respects than they were under the explicit system of racial segregation. Such children face a new form of stigmatization that focuses on test scores and the achievement gap. While it is no longer socially permissible to blame the failure to achieve on race explicitly, a litany of "lacks" (e.g., lack of school readiness, lack of parental support) is used to justify such undereducation and the denial of equal educational opportunity.

This perception of color-blind education effectively eliminates addressing the ideology of inferiority, which undergirds the very foundation of schooling for students from caste minority groups. If it is believed that the ideology of inferiority is no longer a determining factor in the education of students from caste minority groups, then there is no reason to critically analyze the culture and climate of "low-performing" post-*Brown* segregated schools even as this ideology is embedded in the routine policies and practices of these schools.

The belief that education is color-blind makes it possible to avoid suggestions of the "soft bigotry of low expectations," while expressing the notion "that all children can learn" and even promoting high standards for all while still holding beliefs about poor minority students that have emanated from the ideology of inferiority. Ultimately, the perception of color-blind education leads to undesirable outcomes, as it places poor children from caste minority groups at a serious disadvantage by marginalizing the stigmatization under which they labor and denying their differential and often hostile school experiences.

Herein lies one of the major and most critical differences between the pre- and post-*Brown* segregation: the denial of the saliency of race and the failure to acknowledge the sociopolitical context in which schooling from caste minority groups continues to be provided. It is this difference that makes the new segregation most ominous. This denial prevents the employment of any mechanism to help these students transcend the stigmatization imposed by their group membership and prohibits even the possibility of considering such strategies in our reform efforts.

The most damaging aspect of the perception of color-blindness in education is the fact that it is the children themselves who must carry much of the burden of their undereducation. Carrying this burden can have disastrous results. In color-blind post-*Brown* segregated schools, the chronic undereducation, achievement gap, and discipline gap are believed to be the product of the culture and individual failings of the children and their families. The school need assume no responsibility for the failure of these children to be educated.

There are many reasons to be concerned about the resegregation of our nation's schools; one of the most crucial however, is the devastating impact that the "new segregation" is having and will have upon generations of poor children from caste minority groups in the future. It is imperative that we look more closely at what it means to attend a segregated school in the post-*Brown* era.

In part II of this book, the "reality" of the new segregation is examined. In chapters 3 and 4, the culture and climate of post-*Brown* segregated schools are described. And in chapter 5, the impact of stigmatization and color-blind education upon the academic identity, esteem, and aspirations of poor children from caste minorities is addressed.

Part II

SEGREGATION REDESIGNED

3

The Culture of "New" Segregated Schools

You cannot teach a child that you despise.

—James Baldwin

GENERATIONAL MYTHS

A belief is an idea that people assume to be true (Lustig & Koester, 1996). Beliefs are a set of learned interpretations on the basis of which a group can decide what is and what is not logical and correct. Beliefs that are based on or derived from the teachings of those regarded as authorities—such as parents, teachers, preachers, and presidents—and that bestow a sense of privilege or define one's place in the social order are especially difficult to dislodge. Rather, they become "truths" that are transmitted from generation to generation.

STEREOTYPICAL IMAGES

These "truths" are derived from and perpetuated through historical stereo-typical images. Stereotypical images reinforced in the media and pervasive in the larger society infiltrate schools as well. Being a member of a stigmatized group makes even children susceptible to stereotypical images; they are seen not so much as children but as embodiments of the stereotypical adults that they are expected to become. The same images (e.g., unintelligent, lazy, dangerous) held of adults in a stigmatized group are held of the children as well. As a result, poor minority children have the same relationships and same experiences with adults in the school setting as their parents do in the larger society.

Stereotypical images inform the beliefs held about the capacity and character of poor children from caste minority groups. These erroneous beliefs in turn lead to low expectations for the academic achievement and behavior of these children. Most significantly, these beliefs negatively influence the quality of interactions and relationships established between teacher and students. Ultimately the power of stereotypical images and erroneous beliefs creates poor learning environments especially in post-*Brown* segregated schools in which the student's ability to develop an academic identity and motivation to achieve is hampered. Textbox 3.1 illustrates the progression of image to practice.

The same images of inferiority that were attached to historically black segregated schools during the era of Jim Crow are now imposed upon the "new segregated" neighborhood schools. Just the mention of schools located in predominately minority neighborhoods conjure up visions of students of inferior intelligence, out of control, and refusing to learn. As the names of "failing" schools make the front pages of the local paper and are blasted across the television screen on the nightly news, belief in the inferiority of poor minority students is given more credence.

To be assigned to a "failing" school is debilitating in itself. Daily these students must attend schools in which the entire student body is stereotyped as intellectually and culturally inferior. With every failure to make acceptable gains on test scores and improve standing on the "school report card," the inferiority of these schools and the students who attend them is confirmed. While concern is expressed for the poor educational outcomes among poor minority students, consideration is never given to the degradation that must be felt by these students as they daily attend schools in which they are branded as being inferior and know that their failure is expected.

Students who attended pre-*Brown* segregated schools were very much aware of the negative and stereotypical images held of them by the larger society. However, unlike students attending post-*Brown* segregated schools,

---

**Textbox 3.1.   The Progression of Stigmatizing
Images to Stigmatizing Practices**

- Images (stereotyped/distorted)
- Beliefs (erroneous/deficit thinking)
- Expectations (low for academic performance and behavior)
- Practices (stigmatizing)

once they entered the schoolhouse and closed the door behind them, they were presented with and understood a different reality. Whatever society may have thought or believed about them was simply a myth; the image held of them by their teachers and administrators was one of high achievers with unlimited potential.

A CONSTELLATION OF ERRONEOUS BELIEFS

Stereotypical images inform the belief system that provides the context for the schooling of poor minority students in post-*Brown* segregated schools. Cecelski (1996) relates the beliefs expressed by white educators about the black students who would soon desegregate schools in a North Carolina school district. These educators believed that the standards and quality of education for white students would be lowered. They believed that black education was inferior; that black teachers and students were backward because they studied in second-class institutions, albeit designed by Jim Crow laws; and that black teachers had less formal training.

Uniformly low expectations were expressed for the ability of black students. Black students were believed to be unprepared; not to value education; to come from backgrounds that did not instill a desire to learn; and that they were bound to be disorderly in class. The preparation of these educators focused not on debunking these myths about black students but on how to deal with and control the alien blacks who would soon invade their schools.

What is amazing is the persistence and consistency over time of beliefs based upon stereotypical images. The same beliefs held about African American students and used to justify segregation fifty years ago continue to be held of minority students today. Minority students, African American students in particular, are believed (1) to lack intellectual ability, (2) to be unmotivated to learn, and (3) to be undisciplined. This constellation of beliefs negatively impacts the schooling of poor minority students.

These core beliefs:

- Inform the philosophy of education and form the belief systems of schools designated as "low-performing" or "failing."
- Are pervasive in post-*Brown* segregated schools.
- Consistently promote the chronic undereducation of poor children from caste minority groups; if the belief system does not change, the outcomes will remain the same.
- Make it possible for the school (i.e., teachers and administrators) to take no responsibility for the success or failure of students.

- Are an aspect of the "blame the victim" paradigm. Students and their parents are solely blamed for student failure.
- Serve as a major obstacle to the educational achievement of poor students from caste minority groups.
- As in pre-*Brown* segregation, serve as an instrument for denying equal educational opportunity to minority students.

The last twenty years of my professional career have focused on improving educational outcomes for poor and minority, primarily African American students. From 1992 to 1994, that work centered almost exclusively on working with faculties teaching in some twenty to thirty Chapter I (Title I) schools in two urban Florida school districts. These faculties worked in schools located in neighborhoods in which predominately poor blacks (and in a very few cases Latinos) resided.

Before beginning work with each faculty, a simple task was devised to gather information related to images of and beliefs about students in these low-performing schools as well as the reasons the faculty believed were the cause of the low academic performance of students in their schools. The exercise elicited information specifically about images of and beliefs related to race and class.

With movement into the era of "color-blind education" and as schools were becoming resegregated, a shift occurred in the expressed beliefs about minority students and the reasons for their poor academic outcomes. Stereotypical racial images morphed into stereotypical images about class, especially with regard to the poor. Focus shifted from assumed lack of innate intelligence to the "pathology of poverty" and the flawed character traits of both the parent and child.

The comments of teachers in the schools serving primarily poor minority students focused on the "class" and "character." They perceived the "poor" to be unhappy, fearful, anxious, and frustrated. It is the category related to the "character" of the poor that is most telling. The poor were perceived to possess major character flaws. Most often, they were believed to be violent; to engage in criminal activities; to be lazy, shiftless, irresponsible, dirty and dishonest. The poor were perceived to lack good parenting skills, to be unable to make wise decisions, and to be unable to break out of the cycle of poverty.

Some responses from teachers were angry and even mean-spirited; responses included they "don't value life," are "stupid," and are "freeloaders." The term *fertile Myrtles* was used in referring to unwed mothers and the large families of the poor. In true color-blind etiquette, race was rarely used in describing the poor; more often, their character flaws were the focus of criticism.

These teachers also completed a similar exercise related to images of and beliefs held about the middle class. In contrast to the poor, the images of and beliefs about the middle class always included a higher number of positive characteristics as opposed to the predominately negative ones attributed to the poor. The middle class were perceived as being intelligent, white-collar, motivated, hard workers, educated, "involved," and "taxpayers." In most cases, the middle class was also described as being white.

It was principally through this work that a disturbing pattern was identified that was present not only in these schools but in others that served predominately poor minority populations. Without exception, there was a pattern of negative images and beliefs held by teachers in low-achieving schools. Those who hold such images tend to form inaccurate beliefs about the students' ability and to have low expectations of students' academic performance. Ultimately these stereotypical images, erroneous beliefs, and low expectations provide the context for the education of poor minority students in segregated schools; they interfere with and even serve as barriers to the effective education of these students.

TEACHER BELIEFS AND TEACHER POWER

Beliefs rooted in the ideology of inferiority operate in schools at both the individual and the institutional (collective) levels. The beliefs that are held about ourselves and others, especially those from lower socioeconomic and minority groups, are often *unconscious culturally conditioned beliefs* (Bireda, 2010). These beliefs, which operate at a programmed emotional level, affect all of us who have been socialized in this society. Even "good" teachers can unwittingly become the victims of erroneous beliefs based upon this conditioning.

What a teacher believes about a student's capacity to learn and her or his own efficacy as a teacher are crucial to the learning process. When teachers are victims of unconscious culturally conditioned beliefs informed by stereotypical images, not only do they form low expectations of student achievement but, more significantly, they are also robbed of their powers as teachers. Teachers must hold two core sets of beliefs about their students and themselves.

Beliefs about the student:

- I believe in your ability to learn.
- I believe that you have unlimited potential.

Beliefs about self:

- I believe in my capacity to teach you.
- I believe that I have the power to change your life.

Erroneous beliefs based upon stereotypical images held by teachers de-
prive them of belief in their own ability as teachers, diminish their "point
of power," undermine their personal interactions with students, decrease
their power in the classroom, and ultimately contribute to the frustration
and burnout experienced by so many teachers in schools populated by poor
minority students. These erroneous beliefs block such teachers' ability to
see beyond the "image" to really "see" their students—to see their strengths,
talents, gifts, abilities, and potential.

EVIDENCE IGNORED

There has been a sufficient amount of research to provide evidence of
the influence of teacher beliefs and expectations upon student achievement. The seminal study related to teacher expectancy was conducted
during the beginning of the pragmatic desegregation period. The significance of teacher expectancy became widely recognized with Rosenthal and Jacobson's (1968) research and discussion of the "Pygmalion
effect."

Research on the Pygmalion effect demonstrated the relationship between teacher expectation and student performance. When the teacher
was given information that certain students were brighter than others, he
or she behaved in ways to encourage and facilitate student success. The
experiment showed how expectations can affect reality and create self-
fulfilling prophecies.

Daily in classrooms filled with poor black and brown children, teachers' expectations turn into self-fulfilling prophecies. Either consciously or
unconsciously, teacher behavior toward students is based upon beliefs and
assumptions that they hold about them (Bamburg, 1994).

Expectancy research is especially salient with regard to the race and class
of students. Research has clearly shown that low expectations are influenced
by students' race and class backgrounds (Alexander, Entwisle, & Thompson,
1987) and that teachers' perceptions of low-income and African American
students are lower than those held for middle-class and upper-income
white students (Rist, 1970). Most significant in relation to students from
caste minority groups, evidence indicates that students who belong to a
stigmatized group may be particularly vulnerable to self-fulfilling prophecies (Jussim & Harber, 2005).

Despite the evidence showing the relationship between a student's race
and class and teacher expectations and the impact of teacher expectations
upon student achievement, these findings have not been used as the basis
to develop instruments to measure and evaluate teacher expectancy. Also,
while this research has been available for over forty years, reform efforts

---

Textbox 3.2.   The Impact of Teacher Beliefs

If I believe that...	*Then...*
You are not ready for school,	I will not teach you to read.
You possess only deficiencies,	I will not see your strengths.
You have learned nothing,	I will not utilize your transferable skills of value from your environment.
You do not have the aptitude to excel academically,	I will not give you work that challenges you.
You come to school without any cultural capital,	I will not discover your gifts and talents.
You come with "character flaws" because you are poor,	I will not develop a relationship with you.
You lack discipline and self-control,	I will not see or tolerate what is "childlike" in you.
Your parents don't care,	I will not involve them in your education.
Your parents have nothing to offer,	I will not respect them.
You don't want to learn,	I will not teach you.
Your present life condition is your future,	I will take no responsibility if you fail.
I can't teach you,	I will not teach you.

---

have not made teacher expectancy and its impact upon student achievement a focus; rather, reform has continued to be based upon deficit thinking evolving from the ideology of inferiority.

Interestingly as well, Marva Collins became well known as the educator from Chicago who demonstrated the impact of beliefs and expectancy in her work with poor black children. A CBS segment highlighting her work was entitled "Too Good to Be True." Her results obviously were felt to be too good to be true, as her workable methods and strategies are missing from the focus on color-blind standards and test-driven strategies. Perhaps we are so deeply rooted in the ideology of inferiority that we continue to find it inconceivable that poor black and brown children can excel academically. Maybe academic excellence is simply too good to be true for poor minority children.

INSTITUTIONAL BELIEFS

In post-*Brown* segregated schools serving poor minority students, the problem of erroneous beliefs is exacerbated. The attitudes and behavior of individual teachers in a school setting that are based upon erroneous thinking and low expectations can have a very negative impact on students. However, it is disastrous for students when the collective thinking and actions of the teachers and administrators as well as school policies and practices reflect beliefs based upon the ideology of inferiority. This institutionalized belief system characterizes post-*Brown* segregated schools and is a major reason why students attending these schools are chronically undereducated.

In low-performing or failing post-*Brown* segregated schools, the institutionalized beliefs (collective thinking and actions) mean that:

- Inferior educational outcomes are tolerated.
- A pervasive and systematic set of low expectations and standards prevails.
- There is acceptance of and agreement on the label assigned to the school.
- There is a resignation and refusal to challenge or contradict the labels assigned to the students, their parents, and the school.
- There is a commitment to operating within the stigmatizing context (e.g., focusing only on raising test scores while showing no concern for academic excellence).
- There is a "we versus them" stance; a psychological distancing and lack of any emotional connection to the students, their families, or the community that the school serves.
- The "official explanation" or blame for the schools' undereducation of students continues to focus on the faults of the students and parents.
- There is a general dissatisfaction with working in the environment comprising "these students."
- There is an acceptance of a "stigmatizing" school environment as normal and necessary for this particular student population.
- There is a collective lack of responsibility for student learning.

The abdication of responsibility for student outcomes is the most glaring and disturbing characteristic of post-*Brown* segregated schools. The example below illustrates this collective lack of responsibility for student outcomes.

"WHAT IS THE CAUSE OF LOW STUDENT ACHIEVEMENT IN THIS SCHOOL?"

In this rural school district, failure was the norm for African American students. They dropped out early on and usually ended up jobless, in menial labor, or in the criminal justice system. For some reason, African American students appeared doomed almost as soon as they began the educational process. The county in which the school district is located is almost equally divided between blacks and whites, but despite *Brown*, black students attend what is essentially the all-black segregated school, which was the location for the visit.

This elementary school was one with a history of undereducating students. In order to gather some information as to why the faculty believed there was such a dismal record of student achievement, I began by eliciting responses to "What do you believe is the cause of the low student performance in this school?" The responses are ranked in descending order from the highest to the lowest number of times each one appeared.

In descending order, the top five responses of teachers to the question "What do you believe is the cause of low student performance in this school?" were:

- Parents don't get involved.
- Students lack motivation.
- Parents don't care.
- Low socioeconomic status (of students).
- Students' low self-esteem/lack of confidence.

Other comments included lack of discipline, "students don't know the value of education," negative family environments, students' negative mindset, students' lack of readiness skills upon entering kindergarten, lack of verbal skills to communicate effectively, not being able to understand directions, and "no values whatsoever." Two other factors mentioned included domestic violence in the neighborhood and students being exposed to domestic violence in the home.

Not surprisingly, most of the responses focused on the students and parents. Parents carried a large measure of the blame for student failure either as a result of their noninvolvement with the school or because of the home environments they had created. The students themselves, all primary school students, were believed to be most responsible for their academic failure; their lack of motivation, low self-esteem, and lack of skills, along with their poor attitudes and communication skills, were believed to be the source of student failure.

Three teachers finally stepped forward to cite low teacher expectations and administrative instability as school-related factors contributing to low student achievement. It is interesting that these same teachers remarked about the lack of adequate resources and the aesthetics of the campus as contributing factors to current student outcomes. One of these teachers actually voiced the opinion that students coming to this school "had nothing to look forward to," which is probably the most accurate response.

Coming to this school must be a "gut-wrenching" experience for both teachers and students—students being shown daily that there is little hope for them and teachers believing that they have absolutely no power to impact the lives of the students they teach. In this school there is no collective responsibility on the part of professionally trained teachers for student success or failure. It is no wonder that students in this school become disengaged from the schooling process very early. This "story" is repeated over and over in post-*Brown* segregated schools. Poor minority students and their parents are blamed for their chronic undereducation.

Teachers are believed not to have the power to impact a student's life because of family, neighborhood, or the cultural group from which the child comes. While no teacher has the power to effect change in what occurs in a student's home, he or she does have the power to effect change in the student in his or her classroom. This power is relevant and usable only if institutional and individual belief systems allow it. In the majority of post-*Brown* segregated schools, unconscious culturally conditioned beliefs are so pervasive that they serve to undermine the learning experiences of children whose only hope for life change depends upon getting a good education.

Diamond, Randolph, and Spillane (2007) argue that the student composition of schools and what they term the school's "micropolitical context" are closely related. The micropolitical context is described as teachers' beliefs about students' capabilities and their sense of responsibility for student learning. This context is also considered to include the pervasive stream of beliefs, expectations, and practices that flow throughout the school. Their findings indicate that in predominately low-income and African American schools, teachers emphasize students' deficits and have a reduced sense of responsibility for student learning.

As can be expected, students perform better academically in schools and show greater gains where there is a high degree of collective responsibility. In a review of critical factors related to student achievement, Arganbright (1983) finds that in low-achieving schools, staff members generally view their students as being limited in learning ability and do not see themselves as responsible for finding ways to raise students' academic performance. It is exactly this "micropolitical context" that represents a major and critical difference in the culture of pre- and post-*Brown* segregated schools.

The school culture is the belief structure that guides school policies and practices. In post-*Brown* segregated schools, the ideology of intellectual and cultural inferiority undergirds the belief system and serves as a major barrier to the development of student academic identity, esteem, motivation, and achievement. In chapter 4, the climate of schools in which poor students from caste minority groups are chronically undereducated is examined.

4

The Climate of the Post-*Brown* Segregated School

Education represents a central experience in life.

—Earl Warren, *Brown v. Board of Education*, 1954

Two women were discussing their observations of black children on their way home from the predominately white school that they attended. They were troubled by the demeanor of the students, especially the boys who walked with their heads down and shoulders slumped. One commented, "I told you, black kids can't develop self-esteem in white schools."

That discussion is one that has been taking place among African Americans since the desegregation of schools. But before a rush to judgment and the assumption that a return to all-black schools is the answer, it must be understood that black and brown children will fare poorly in either predominately white or predominately minority schools in which they suffer any form of stigmatization. Poor minority students who attend segregated neighborhood schools with stigmatizing environments will suffer both academically and emotionally.

STIGMATIZING SCHOOL ENVIRONMENTS

Besides the usual inequities in facilities and resources, there are sharp and perceptible differences in the "feel" or climates of schools attended by the white middle class and those that poor minority students attend. In many segregated schools attended by poor minority students, there is an undercurrent of tension and, in some cases, a sense of fear on the part of staff.

This "feel" is the result most often of stereotypical images (e.g., "out of control," "violent") held of the students who attend the schools. In many cases, the teachers and administrators in these schools react and respond to the stereotypical images rather than the actual students.

A school's climate is a reflection of the values, beliefs, and perceptions of the student population. As evidenced in chapter 3, the education of poor children from caste minority groups is viewed through a prism of lack, incapacity, and inferiority. These stereotypical images and erroneous beliefs are translated into school environments which negatively impact the academic, emotional, and social development of the students that attend them. The environments in these "low-performing" schools are *stigmatizing environments* that are shaped by the racial and class stereotypes held by the larger society and perpetuate them. These *stigmatizing environments* serve as a major *institutional* barrier to the achievement of the students who attend such schools.

What is a *stigmatizing school environment*? It is one in which a set of institutional beliefs rooted in the ideology of inferiority limit the learning potential of students, construct institutional barriers to achievement, and deny *students* an equal educational opportunity. In post-*Brown* segregated schools where poor educational outcomes are the norm, stereotypical images and erroneous beliefs translate into environments that stigmatize and negatively impact not only the academic but also the emotional and social development of students.

In stigmatizing school environments, erroneous beliefs operate not only at the individual level but permeate the entire schooling context. Every aspect of the school environment—from patterns of communication, relationships, the formal and informal curriculum and instructional strategies, to policies and practices that govern the school—is affected. Students in stigmatizing environments receive negative messages about their value and their abilities, which ultimately influence not only their performance but attitudes toward the schooling process itself.

In stigmatizing environments, the nurturing, encouraging relationships especially needed by poor students from caste minority groups are virtually nonexistent; in fact, students are often subject to psychological maltreatment. Hyman and Snook (1999) describe some elements of psychological maltreatment in schools, all of which are manifested in stigmatizing environments:

- Low quality of human interaction in which teachers communicate a lack of interest, caring, and affection for students through ignoring, isolation, and rejection
- Limited opportunities for students to develop adequate skills and feelings of self-worth

- Encouragement to be dependent and subservient
- Denial of opportunities for healthy risk taking such as exploring ideas that are not conventional and approved by the teacher
- Exposing children to systematic bias and prejudice

A CENTRAL LIFE EXPERIENCE

The school experience is said to be one that can shape an individual for the better or the worse. If the school experience is nurturing, challenging, and encouraging, the student will usually develop the confidence and skills that foster success in life. If however, only failure, frustration, and shame are experienced, then the student will find school to be such a negative experience that the discomfort felt is not worth any future rewards that schooling might bring. Because of the life-altering impact an education can have on a child from a caste minority group, a positive and high-quality schooling experience is crucial.

The theory of psychosocial development outlined by Erikson (1968) affirms the central place that the school experience has in the life and future development of children. According to Erikson, the period during which children attend elementary school (ages six to eleven) is socially a most decisive stage. It is during this period that children develop either a *sense of industry* or a *sense of inferiority*.

In order to be successful in this stage, which means developing a sense of *competency*, certain elements must be present in the learning environment and the child's school experience. If she is given an opportunity to make and do things, to acquire the basic skills needed to feel competent, and her efforts are praised and encouraged, she will develop a sense of industry. If, however, she is limited in the activities in which she can engage, does not acquire the skills that will make her feel competent, and is not encouraged but rather criticized and even denigrated, she will develop a sense of inferiority.

As stated earlier, the quality of the learning environment and school experience is critical for poor students from caste minority groups. It is exactly during this period, in the elementary years that many of these students disengage from the schooling process. By the end of the third grade and probably earlier, their school experiences have contributed to a loss of confidence in their abilities; thus they give up on the only institution that can help to change their life conditions and improve their life chances.

In a stigmatizing school environment, which is described in great detail below, the two elements required for students to develop a sense of competency and confidence in their abilities are missing. In the academic milieu, the opportunities to participate in an expansive set of learning opportunities is not available, and the social milieu is often void of the nurturing and encouraging relationships so needed by the children who attend these schools. In the sections that follow, a glimpse of what the learning environments and school experiences are like for poor minority children who attend post-*Brown* segregated schools is provided.

THE HIDDEN CURRICULUM

Anyon's research (1980), described in detail below, provides evidence of how schools perpetuate the class system by providing different types of knowledge and educational experiences for children of different socioeconomic groups. Anyon examined the curricula and educational experiences of fifth graders in five elementary schools in four contrasting school communities. These studies involved two "working class" schools; one "middle-class" school; one "affluent professional" school; and one "executive elite" school. The social class designation was derived from parents' occupations and family income.

Anyon's findings indicate that there is a "hidden curriculum" that prepares students from different social classes for "class-specific" roles in society. In essence, the school experiences of working-class students prepared them for jobs that were routine and mechanical in nature, while upper-class students were prepared for jobs that demand creativity and skills of self-management.

Anyon found that "work" in the working-class schools meant following the steps of a procedure that was usually mechanical, involving rote behavior and very little decision making. Work was evaluated not so much on whether it was right or wrong but according to whether the children followed the right steps. Students were told exactly what to do and no attempt was made to relate the steps to a thought process or larger context. Control of the students' time, space, and movement was very important in the working-class context.

The middle-class experience differed in that work in this context involved "getting the right answer." In this case, that called for following directions involving some decision making. It was important, however, for middle-class students to gain some level of understanding of the material, although most lessons were based on the textbook. Work tasks for middle-class students did not require critical thinking or creativity. Very important in the middle-class context was following external rules and regulations.

In the affluent professional context, work was "creative activity" carried out independently. In this context, ideas, critical thinking, and decision making were the norm. Students were continually asked to express and apply ideas and concepts. Their work involved individual thought as well as the expression, expansion, and illustration of ideas. Material products such as written stories, essays, murals, and crafts were evaluated on quality of expression and appropriateness of the conception to the task. Students in the affluent professional schools were praised, provided with suggestions, given freedom of movement, and allowed to engage in negotiation regarding some classroom activities.

Work in the executive elite school involved developing one's analytical and intellectual powers. Students were required to reason through problems and produce intellectual products of top academic quality. These students were involved in critical thinking, decision making, discussion of concepts, and independent research. Interestingly, in the executive elite context, the discussion of concrete social issues and problems was allowed. Student opinions were valued and students were instructed that "it is not enough to get it right on the test; you must use what you learn." Finally, there was little attempt to regulate the movement of these students; instead, self-regulation was stressed.

Anyon's research shows that the school experiences in the schools sampled differed qualitatively by social class. These differences, according to Anyon (1980), not only contribute to the development in the children of each social class of certain economically significant relationships but also help to reproduce the systems of relations in the society. Anyon's study can help to provide some interesting insights as we explore the quality of education received by poor minority children in post-*Brown* segregated schools.

Most significantly for this discussion, Anyon's study involved a predominately white sample. While the working-class student population is educated in a "class-oriented" context, they are still "privileged with whiteness" in this society and are not burdened by the stigma of innate inferiority. If working-class white children are subjected to a hidden curriculum that potentially limits their roles in society, how much more deleterious must be the impact of being schooled in an environment where you are predetermined to be intellectually and culturally inferior.

The "hidden" class-based pedagogy provided for students attending post-*Brown* segregated schools is caste education. The original intent and purpose of caste education, as stated earlier, was to maintain a subservient class and prevent open competition in the job market. Resegregated schools adeptly serve the purpose of implementing the caste education initially designed for black students but circumvented by African American teachers in pre-*Brown* segregated schools. The curriculum and educational experiences provided poor minority students are similar to those of white working-class students in Anyon's study but with the added element of institutional stigmatization.

STIGMATIZING SCHOOL ENVIRONMENTS
AND CASTE EDUCATION

The two major characteristics of stigmatizing environments are the implementation of a "culture of control" (Cortes, 2010) and of a "practical" curriculum (Anyon, 1980). The outstanding feature of a stigmatizing school environment, which can immediately be seen and felt upon entering the school, is the strong orientation of discipline versus academics. Hallways and classroom walls are filled with signs that post rules and admonishments to behave as well as the ubiquitous character education posters. Because of the perception and belief that poor minority students are undisciplined and out of control, very high standards are held for what is considered to be appropriate behavior.

The strict conformity and obedience required in these stigmatizing environment are designed to ensure that students develop the personality traits and attitudes conducive to taking orders, following directions, and being compliant in menial work situations. Self-expression, individuality, and "getting out of line" or "forgetting your place" are not tolerated. Students who rebel against the sense of powerlessness induced in this environment more often than not experience disciplinary problems.

Test-driven reforms have made the stigmatizing environment even more destructive. Academic excellence has been sacrificed to produce higher test scores and better ratings for schools. Test-oriented instruction has meant a further deterioration of the type and quality of instruction received by students attending low-performing segregated schools. The paucity of meaningful academic content makes the need to control students greater as schooling becomes an increasingly boring and frustrating venture. Students subjected to this type of testing regime also experience a perpetual state of stereotype threat.

Students are provided with a limited knowledge base and skill set for the sole purpose of passing tests. Students in these schools are in a perpetual testing mode; practice tests, pretests, and the "real" test. They follow a set pattern of being presented with material for the test, copying the material, memorizing the material, and being tested. According to Baker (2006), this reliance on standardized tests has produced educational outcomes that are increasingly problematic and actually limit opportunities for most African American students.

The "practical" curriculum is not intended to advance educational excellence or to prepare poor minority students for upward mobility. A focus on what is adequate for a given grade level rather than expanding the educational horizons of students is the norm. The sense of competency and confidence that comes from exploration, discovery, and being involved in creative pursuits is denied these students.

Finally, the standards and test-driven focus have also resulted in a retreat from acknowledging and addressing the unique needs of students from caste minority groups. Focus on the affective domain, especially crucial to the intellectual and social development of students from caste minority groups, is noticeably absent.

Below are examples of the types of curricula and educational experiences that are provided students attending post-*Brown* segregated and low-achieving schools. These schools are given the names Central City Elementary and Riverside High School. They illustrate the types of curriculums and educational experiences that are provided to students attending post-*Brown* segregated and low-achieving schools.

CENTRAL CITY ELEMENTARY SCHOOL

Central City Elementary sits in the heart of the downtown section of a city characteristic of the "old South." Of the 300 students who attend this "inner-city" school, 99 percent are African American, live in a public housing project a few blocks away, and are designated to receive free or reduced-cost lunches. The school has for some time been unable to raise its "below-average improvement" rating.

The Academic Milieu

The focus of instruction at Central City, as at other "low-performing" schools, is to boost test scores. Reading is, of course, central to reaching this goal. Students are engaged in some type of reading activity (i.e., independent, group, accelerated reader, group discussion of stories, or worksheets) each day. They finish their assigned tasks and take diagnostic tests. It is certainly not the concentration on reading itself that is problematic but the routine almost factory-oriented, assembly-line fashion in which it occurs. There is no room for thinking or moving outside of the box.

Opportunities for "real" learning that take place and promote a sense of competency through discovery, exploration, risk taking, and creative endeavors do not exist in this environment. The excitement of learning is absent and there is, in a sense, a denial of freedom to pursue academic excellence. In one second-grade classroom, it appeared that a student diagnosed with Asperger's syndrome, who seemed to know every conceivable fact about U.S. presidents, was the only student in the classroom who was actually free to pursue his passion.

This school was expected soon to become a magnet school for global studies in order to attract the children of the middle- and upper-class whites who lived in nearby areas and those of professionals who worked downtown. But the "magnet school" concept inherently promotes the ideology of inferiority. Essentially, the message conveyed is that a caste education is appropriate and good enough for poor minority children but that only the privileged children of the affluent professional class are entitled to a world-class education. The types of educational opportunities used to entice middle-class white parents to send their children to inner-city schools should always be afforded the children who already attend these schools.

That being said, hopefully the poor minority children who attend this school will reap some of the benefits of having white and middle-class students among them. However, in reality, simply adding a new curriculum will not necessarily benefit the poor minority children attending this school unless there are major changes in their social milieu.

The Social Milieu

There appear to be two distinct reactions to the children who attend this high-poverty school: pity and scorn. Daily, the school is filled with volunteers demonstrating an almost "missionary zeal" who are determined to help these poor, underprivileged children. They shuffle about, removing students from classes in order to offer extra help with reading and providing after-school enrichment programs. While a flurry of activity surrounds the school and students here receive plenty of extra attention, the most important element in terms of meeting the educational needs of these students and improving educational outcomes is missing.

While students have positive relationships with the volunteers, the most critical relationships, those with their teachers, are lacking. The images of and beliefs held about the children by the teachers negatively impact their ability to establish the relationships that these students need. In this school and others like it serving poor minority children, the images of poor black children and the beliefs that flow from them determine the quality of the affective environment in which the children are expected to learn.

It is during the elementary school years that the child's budding academic identity is being formed. It is bolstered by a sense of competency, which comes with the acquisition of skills and with encouragement and praise from the teacher. The development of an academic identity is also strongly influenced by the messages the student receives in the school environment; messages about his worth and abilities. Thus the development of a positive academic identity will lead to achievement motivation and high academic aspirations.

The teacher–student relationship is extremely crucial to children from caste minority groups. From this relationship, they seek and need to feel that they are valued and that their abilities are affirmed. The teacher is the one person who, in the mind of the student, can dispel all of the negative stereotypes held about him in the larger society. Several studies, such as those described below, support the strong need for teacher approval among students form caste minority groups, including African American students.

Ferguson (1998) suggests that black students are more "teacher dependent" than white students. Holliday (1985) studied the extent to which and the process whereby teacher and child perceptions influence children's achievement. Holliday found that the teacher's perceptions were highly related to black students' achievement, and she speculated that some teacher attitudes could transform some black children's achievement efforts into learned helplessness effects. Zimmerman, Khoury, Vega, Gil, and Wahrheit (1995) found that student perceptions of the respect, interest, and support received from their teachers significantly influenced their academic motivation, effort, and achievement. The warmth and concern of some teachers is overshadowed by the yelling, harshness, sarcasm, and public humiliation of students by others. While the students in this school appeared to be pretty normal kids who act the way children act at this age, their misbehavior was the major focus of teachers' attention. Discussions with teachers did not elicit discussions about student academic progress; instead, teachers' major concerns involved discipline and decorum. Comments such as " they lack common etiquette" and " they have tendencies toward rude behavior" were voiced.

Like the teachers in Anyon's study of working-class schools, the control of student movement was of primary concern. Teachers complained about students not sitting correctly in their seats, getting up and walking around without permission, and talking out of turn. Images of students who come from poor families and beliefs about them appeared to have a powerful influence in the school. In many instances, the teachers who were most harsh and disrespectful of students were themselves African American.

RIVERSIDE HIGH SCHOOL

While pity is a major response to the poor black students who attend Central City Elementary, feelings of disdain for the students and a sense of the need to control them is most pervasive at Riverside High School. Upon arrival, the cleanliness of the building, the sense of order, and the reports of progress made toward steadily increasing test scores is impressive. With each succeeding day however, it is obvious that this school is a perfect example of the stigmatizing environment of caste education that is being provided to a predominately African American population. The students attending this school are being prepared to take low-paying jobs involving clerical work or the jobs in the service industry or to go into military service.

Riverside High School is a rural, 96 percent African American school serving grades 9 through12. Of the approximately 400 students who attend the school, 87 percent receive free or reduced-cost lunches. The enrollment has steadily declined over the past several years, as students who are able have transferred to other schools in the district.

In stigmatizing environments, there is usually a contradiction between the stated and expressed or demonstrated beliefs about students. For instance, two of the "core" stated beliefs espoused by teachers at Riverside are "Students should be actively involved in solving problems and producing quality work" and "Students learn in different ways and should be provided a variety of instructional approaches to support their learning." However, the culture of control that permeates the school prevents either of these beliefs from being demonstrated in the learning environment at Riverside.

The teachers' expressed beliefs about students at Riverside are a good indicator of what the climate is like there. When teachers were asked to describe the students who attend Riverside, the following were among their responses:

- Obnoxious
- Immature
- Not scholarly
- Have issues
- Lazy
- Unmotivated
- Apathetic
- Need parents with common sense

The general institutional belief is that Riverside students lack potential and character. They are expected to drop out of school or, if they graduate, to join the military or take menial jobs in the area.

Academic Milieu

Riverside is definitely a test-driven school. Students are involved in preparing for or taking one of four major assessments throughout the school year. A "data wall," which prominently displays the rankings for each assessment, is a constant reminder to students of the reason that they attend school. It appears that "testing burnout" is now occurring; students are reported to be sleeping or talking during testing. Even with this focus, there are only slight improvements in student performance: the school has moved from an "unsatisfactory" to a "below average" rating. Even more significantly, 82 percent of females but only 53 percent of males (an increase from previous years) graduated in the last year.

Students take the standard course offerings, including also Honors English and Algebra II. Freshmen take a "boot camp"–like Freshman Seminar, and there are a few electives, including Spanish I and II; Keyboarding, Business and Personal Finance, Business Communication, Parenting Education, Food Nutrition, Culinary Arts, and Driver Education. The most obvious indicator of the institutional belief system is the lack of rigor in coursework. Students are simply not challenged and as a result are terribly undereducated.

As can be expected, work in classes follows a predictable routine: lecture, copy notes from Smart Board, memorize, take test. Students complain of being bored and as a result often act out their frustration. There is a total absence of any opportunities for students to engage in critical thinking. These students, who are obviously victims of social inequities, will acquire absolutely no skills that will help them interpret, analyze, or question their life situations or to engage in problem solving related to social issues.

Most amazing, considering the momentous occasion of an African American running for and being inaugurated as president, there were no mock elections and no discussions related to the presidential contest during the entire campaign. Finally, despite the symbolism of the occasion, students were not allowed to watch the inauguration of the president. Current events are summarized and reacted to on dittoed sheets rather than discussed in class. The reason given for the inability for students to engage in cooperative learning or any group activities is that teachers are fearful of losing control of the class.

While college attendance is mentioned, the environment does not promote the notion of college attendance; there is a much greater focus on students going to the military as a way out of poverty rather than using their education for that purpose. There are, in fact, aspects of the educational experience at Riverside that work against college attendance.

First of all, there are no opportunities for the development of leadership skills (the reasons for this are discussed below). Student government exists in name only. Students have no decision-making power or influence over student life at the school whatsoever; all authority is in the hands of the administration. "Club day" is held once per month, with students being assigned to a club or spending the hour in a "holding cell" located in the gymnasium. The "holding cell" is a derogatory name given to the area in which students who were not assigned to a club spend the club hour. Students are warned constantly that if they are found in the halls or if the hour is not conducted properly, they will lose club day.

Club meetings consist of teachers talking to students; there is no student control or leadership involved. In addition, there are no opportunities to earn points (required for most colleges now) for volunteering and service learning opportunities. As such, students who do choose to go to college are limited in their choice of college owing to the lack of educational experiences that could give them the needed minimal skills. Again, Career Day is very limited, with the military being the major focus.

Social Milieu

Riverside High School fits what Contes (2010) terms the "command and control" model. The institutional belief that the students attending this school lack self-discipline and must be tightly controlled accounts for the overarching focus on discipline and control. This involves the control of every aspect of student life: student movement, student expression, and the types of learning experiences in which students can engage. The major focus of the student handbook is discipline, and consequences for offenses are detailed. This focus has given the school the distinction of being the school with the highest number of suspensions in the district.

Discussions at faculty meetings focus on two major topics: increasing test scores and, of course, student discipline. Teachers are exhorted to consistently enforce the "top ten"—a list of offenses including failing to wear one's ID badge or wearing sagging pants, improper uniforms or head coverings; having one's shirt untucked; using the wrong book bags; bringing food or drinks into the classroom; chewing gum; using electronic gadgets; and being outside the classroom without a hall pass. This is certainly not meant to be diatribe against appropriate student conduct and order but rather an appeal for balance and reason in schools as well as a caution against letting stereotypical images govern the educational experiences of poor minority students.

Finally, one would think that nurturing relationships and personal attention would be the norm in a high school with only 400 students. At Riverside High School, as in other schools with stigmatizing environments, images of and beliefs about students serve as barriers to teachers forming the type of relationships that students need. The lack of the "practice of caring" is the most glaring characteristic of Riverside High School and other predominately minority schools with stigmatizing school environments.

Anger among students at Riverside High School is common. They complain of being bored and frustrated in classes. Students believe that teachers do not manage their classes, do not have patience with them, do not explain information well, do not answer their questions, and do not make sure that they learn. They generally believe that in many classes they are not learning anything. Most of all, they believe that their teachers do not care.

Studies indicate that lack of teacher caring and lack of teacher–peer respect contribute to underachievement among black students.

Ferguson (1998) found that strong, supportive teacher–student relationships may be critical resources for black and Hispanic students and that teacher encouragement is of distinctive importance as a source of motivation for nonwhite students. Finally, Zimmerman and colleagues (1995) found that students' perceptions of teacher disinterest are directly related to feelings of alienation, lack of commitment to school, and drop-out rates among low-socioeconomic-status minority students.

Interestingly, the faculty acknowledge that they face challenges in terms of improving student achievement. They suggest that more challenging, rigorous, standards-based instruction; more active engagement of students; and more students eagerly accepting the challenge of high expectations would improve student outcomes. However, they do not see the relationship between the negative institutional beliefs held of students, the total focus on testing rather than educating students, the oppressive environment of control and poor student outcomes.

It is ironic that in preparing for an accreditation visit, teachers were encouraged to "teach an engaging lesson" and to "make their rooms look attractive." Perhaps, if these behaviors were the norm, the academic environment of Riverside would change.

Stigmatizing environments foster the implementation of caste education. They limit the acquisition of knowledge, skills, and attitudes conducive to high academic achievement. Stigmatizing environments produce poor educational outcomes that directly contribute to the "achievement gap" and for which the students themselves are blamed (see textboxes 4.1 and 4.2).

Current standards and test-driven reforms contribute to the caste education of poor minority students as well as—by restricting the knowledge base to which they are exposed, the acquisition of strategic skills, and the development of personal traits such as creativity, initiative, assertiveness—ultimately sabotaging their ability to improve their life chances. They are deprived of the tools they would need to achieve upward mobility and to secure social power in this society.

Ogbu (1978) suggests that this is a mechanism by which black students are socialized to develop personal qualities of dependence, compliance, and manipulation while white students, on the other hand, are socialized to develop personal qualities of independence, initiative, industriousness, and individualistic competitiveness. In this way, the public school system reinforces the inferior education of blacks and the superior education of whites.

As strategies to close the achievement gap and improve educational outcomes for poor minority students have been debated and sought, the one aspect of schooling that may hold answers has been sorely overlooked. Typically, finding new ways to treat and change these children and their parents has been the norm, while the environments in which poor minority children must learn have remained off limits as a possible source contributing to the problem of their poor educational outcomes.

In this age of color-blind education, it is politically incorrect to seek any solution that is not data-driven, and administrators who attempt to address issues within the school environment related to race and class often face repercussions. However, Jackson (1999) suggests that the environment in which African American children are schooled should be considered and examined as an important source of risk for the developmental outcomes suffered by these children.

In light of what occurs in stigmatizing environments where caste education is the dominant pedagogy, it may reasonably be concluded that the undereducation of poor students from caste minority groups is deliberate and that the "achievement gap" hype is only a subterfuge to reinforce the ideology of inferiority and to perpetuate the caste system. It would seem that the undereducation of these children, rather than the achievement gap, should be the major focus at this point.

Textbox 4.1.   Characteristics of Stigmatizing Learning Environments

- Culture of control
- Restrictive, class-based curriculum
- Psychological maltreatment
- Poor teacher–student relationships
- Lack of opportunities to develop a sense of competence or confidence in academic abilities
- Lack of opportunities to develop the social capital needed for upward mobility

---

Textbox 4.2.   The Relationship between Stigmatizing Environments and the Achievement Gap

- Stigmatizing environment (based on ideology of inferiority)
- Caste education (culture of control/ practical curriculum)
- Undereducation (inadequate knowledge base/skills/attitudes)
- Poor educational outcomes (input = output)
- "Achievement gap"/perpetuation of caste system ("blaming the victim")

5

The Impact of Stigmatization

The reform efforts aimed at improving the academic performance of students from caste minority groups have focused on solutions that do not threaten the prevailing structure of education for these students. It is interesting and telling that while there has been essentially a return to a racially segregated school system, the proposed solutions in no way acknowledge the evidence that heavily influenced the Supreme Court's decision in *Brown v. Board of Education*.

During the 1940s, Drs. Kenneth and Mamie Clark used dolls to study children's attitudes toward race. Their findings were presented as evidence by the NAACP Legal Defense Fund to show that black children suffered from low self-esteem as a result of the stigma that accompanied racial segregation. Boykin and Jones (2004) suggest the implication that racially separate facilities are detrimental to black children was one of the important legacies of the *Brown* decision.

While racial stigmatization is as detrimental to children from caste minority groups now as it was fifty years ago, the issue has received scant or no attention. To date, there has been a failure to address the potential impact of racial and class stigmatization upon the students who attend low-performing schools. More importantly, there has been an utter failure to investigate the impact of stigmatizing school environments upon the educational attainment of these students.

It has been established that students who attend post-*Brown* segregated schools come from caste minority groups and are schooled differently than their middle-class peers. It should come as no surprise, considering the stigmatizing environments in which they are schooled, that poor minority students are chronically undereducated. Fischer and colleagues

(1996) argue that educational outcomes are related to a group's status in society and that groups score unequally on tests because they are unequal in society. As the research demonstrates, in any society where inequality prevails, unequal educational outcomes are to be expected; this nation is no exception.

The schooling experiences and educational outcomes for students from low-caste groups are similar all over the world. International studies provide ample evidence of the relationship between low-caste status and school performance. In this chapter, international studies related to caste status and educational attainment are examined, as well as the impact of caste minority status on educational achievement in this country.

CASTE MINORITY STATUS AND EDUCATIONAL ATTAINMENT

Caste minority status has been found to be a determining factor in a group's educational attainment. Ogbu (1978) and Gibson and Ogbu (1991) studied majority and minority groups belonging to the same and different races. Their findings confirmed that social status—especially belonging to a low-caste group—more than race was the determining factor in educational achievement and that a change in social status can improve the educational outcomes for a previously low-caste group.

For instance, the Burakumin, racially the same as the dominant Japanese population, are an outcaste minority group in Japan, where they are considered to be mentally and morally inferior. Students from this group are overly represented in prevocational rather than academic courses and in special education; truancy and school dropouts are prevalent in this group. When, however, the Burakumin immigrated to the United States and became voluntary minorities rather than members of a caste minority, their school performance changed. In the United States, this group experiences scholastic success; those remaining in Japan continue to demonstrate low academic performance.

Likewise, West Indians born in Britain have educational experiences similar to those of African Americans in the United States. They are subject to low teacher expectations and are disproportionately represented in special education classes and underrepresented in selective schools. When, however, West Indian students immigrate to the United States and become members of a voluntary minority rather than a caste minority, they demonstrate high academic success. Ogbu (1978) describes an immigrant minority as a group that has voluntarily moved into the host society and operates outside the beliefs of an established system of social hierarchy. Immigrant minorities are not generally considered by the dominant group in the host society to be intellectually or culturally inferior.

Overall, the results of the international studies conducted by Ogbu (1978) and Gibson and Ogbu (1991) indicate that:

- The school performance of caste-like minorities is significantly influenced by the caste-like stratification system.
- There is a wide gap in educational achievement—for example, in cognitive skills, scholastic achievement, and level of academic mastery—between the minority and dominant groups.
- The common factor among the caste groups studied was that there is a subordinate relationship with the dominant group; there was a history of denigration, exclusion, and unequal educational and economic opportunities.
- The history of the caste minority group was found to have a direct bearing on the perceptions, interpretations, and responses of schooling on both students and parents.
- The same patterns of low academic achievement and high drop-out rates were found among caste minorities abroad as well as in the United States.

Differences between first- and second-generation voluntary minorities in the United States also highlight the significant impact of self-perception and being perceived by others as a caste minority rather than a voluntary minority. Both second-generation Mexican Americans and West Indian students perform less well than their first-generation counterparts (Gibson & Ogbu, 1991). Voluntary minorities (immigrants) were also found to experience a greater degree of academic success than involuntary (caste) minorities of similar social class background. It was concluded that teachers hold higher expectations for the academic achievement of voluntary minorities and develop more positive relationships with these students than with caste minorities.

Another international study by Lee (1991) provides evidence of the powerful influence of expectations upon student achievement. According to Lee, the experiences of Koreans in Japan and the United States have important implications for low-status groups such as African Americans. The educational outcomes of Koreans in Japan are similar to those of African Americans in the United States. Lee's work shows that a minority group can have very different achievement patterns in different host countries.

In Japan, Korean students attend lower-class schools; they have more discipline problems and high delinquency rates. Japanese teachers hold low expectations for Korean students because of their negative attitudes toward Korean culture. Lee (1991) suggests that peers observe teacher expectations, hold lower expectations for the group, and as a result create the conditions for distraction by the peer group. In addition, because of their status in society, parents also hold low expectations for their children. As a result of teacher, peer group, and parent expectations, students actualize their low self-expectations into low achievement.

In the United States, Korean students usually attend middle-class schools and are perceived by their teachers to be high academic achievers. Teachers have positive attitudes toward Asian cultural characteristics; as a result, peer groups have high educational expectations, and Korean students in the United States, unlike their peers in Japan, actualize high educational self-expectations into high academic achievement.

IMPLICATIONS OF INTERNATIONAL STUDIES FOR POST-*BROWN* SEGREGATED SCHOOLS

There is much that can be learned from international studies focusing on caste minority status and educational outcomes that can be beneficial in transforming the education of poor minority students in the United States. Ogbu (1978) suggests that the ideology of equality of opportunity through education, which is based primarily on the experiences of the dominant group, does not take into consideration the relationship between the dominant and minority group that is based upon the principle of caste. Ogbu asserts that while language, culture, and poverty do influence school performance, these factors by themselves do not necessarily lead to school failure; lower school performance of caste minorities is adapted to their caste-like status.

Among students from caste minority groups in the United States, Ogbu (1978) found a tendency toward *mental withdrawal* or *academic disengagement* that begins somewhere between the third and sixth grades. Students from these groups begin to manifest boredom, inattentiveness, effort deficits, and discipline problems. Considering the stigmatizing environments in which they are schooled, this actually should come as no surprise. Gibson and Ogbu (1991) also contend that remedial programs and educational reform movements have been ineffective with students from caste minority groups.

This being the case, teachers and administrators in post-*Brown* segregated schools would do well to consider:

- Caste minority status, no matter the stated ideals of the society, negatively impacts educational outcomes.
- In whatever society they reside, students who are members of caste minority groups have the same school experiences, which include stereotyping, low expectations, and differential treatment.
- Academic disengagement and negative peer attitudes are predictable outcomes for students from caste minority groups as a result of their school experiences.

- When the school experiences—images held, beliefs about students, and expectations for those from caste minorities—change, educational outcomes for these students will change as well.
- Educational reform efforts will continue to fail for the masses of students from caste minority groups until we acknowledge and address issues related to caste minority status and its impact.

STEREOTYPE THREAT

A major impact of the stigma associated with caste minority membership has been examined in recent studies. Steele and Aronson (1995) identified *stereotype threat* as a mechanism that contributes to the poor test performance of minority groups. This term refers to the fear that one will be evaluated based upon the negative stereotype associated with the group to which one belongs.

Steele and Aronson (1995) investigated the existence and consequences of stereotype threat in four experiments involving African American and white college students. Their findings indicated that African American participants:

- Performed less well than their white counterparts in the stereotype threat condition but their performance equaled that of whites in non-threat conditions
- Completed fewer test items and had less success in correctly answering items under stereotype threat conditions
- Showed heightened awareness of racial identity and had more doubts about their ability in threat conditions
- Performed less well when racial identity was salient prior to testing

These studies with African American college students, members of a caste minority, provided evidence that performance in academic contexts can be harmed by the awareness that one's behavior might be evaluated in terms of racial stereotypes. If African American college students are victims of the effects of stereotype threat, it can only be assumed that the effect will be greater upon students in stigmatizing environments who are subject to persistent high-stakes testing and who have not yet developed an academic identity or confidence in their academic abilities.

THE BLUE-EYED/BROWN-EYED EXPERIMENT

The most revealing examination of the impact of stigmatization upon students' emotional states, behavior, and academic performance was the blue-eyed/brown-eyed experiment conducted by Jane Elliot, a teacher, in the late 1960s and 1970s (Peters, 1987). Elliot's daring exercise, designed to teach her third-grade students about discrimination, provides a powerful lesson on the effects of stigmatization.

Elliot used eye color as the criterion for determining who would belong to the stigmatized and privileged groups. On the first day, brown-eyed children were declared to be superior and privileged students while and blue-eyed students were stigmatized. On the next day, the roles were reversed. On days that students were labeled as "inferior," they began to look, feel, and behave like inferior students. Their behavior and schoolwork deteriorated. When students were labeled as "superior," they excelled in their schoolwork. The only difference in a student's performance in a superior or inferior manner was his or her assigned status.

Elliot described an "unexpected effect on learning" from the experiment. Students labeled inferior were barely able to perform, while those labeled superior did exceptional work. Elliot found that without exception, students' scores went up on the day they were labeled superior and down when they were labeled inferior. Elliot suggests that when the students were in the superior group, they genuinely did superior work because "they find out for the first time what their true potential is. The children's expectations of themselves changed."

This experiment also demonstrates the power of the teacher's words. When asked by Elliot why, when labeled inferior, the students believed her, they responded that "they believed her because she said so, because I was the teacher." The teacher's words had a far-reaching impact on the group labeled "superior" as well. They observed the inferior quality of work produced by students labeled inferior and started to treat their peers as though they were in fact inferior.

What is remarkable and most significant about Elliot's experiment is that it was conducted in an all-white school in Iowa. While these third-grade students had little or no previous contact with minorities, they were very much aware of the stigmatized groups in society—blacks and Native Americans, for example. They knew the stereotypes of these groups ("dumb people") and understood that they were treated differently; "they don't get anything," one student remarked.

Being subjected to stigmatization was traumatic for white students accustomed to privilege. It is significant that these white children, having endured the pain of stigmatization for only a day, exhibited all the behaviors frequently seen among poor minority students, such as depression, anger, aggressive behavior, and poor academic performance. If, in the span of two afternoons, the emotional health, behavior, and academic performance of privileged white children could be altered, it is absolutely necessary for educators to question the impact of the cumulative effect of stigmatization upon poor minority children.

The students in Elliot's experiment wore "collars" to designate their inferior status. The students described what it felt like to be labeled as inferior. "I felt down, unhappy, like I couldn't do anything; like I was tied up and couldn't get loose." The most revealing expression of what it must feel like to be stigmatized came from Ray, one of the male students. When asked "How did you feel yesterday?" He replied, "Like a dog on a leash. Like you're chained up in a prison, and they threw the key away."

Poor minority children consistently wear collars that represent their race and class. Unlike the children in Elliot's experiment, however, they are unable to discard their collars in the larger society or at school. In school, these students are trapped in a perpetually stigmatizing situation from which there is no escape unless they drop out or are forced out of school.

IMPLICATIONS OF ELLIOT'S EXPERIMENT

Elliot's experiment has significant implications for schools labeled as "low performing" and "failing." Labeling students and the schools they attend as inferior and treating them as such flies in the face of any efforts to raise their achievement levels. Among the lessons we can learn from this experiment are the following:

- The verbal and nonverbal messages sent by the teacher have a powerful influence upon the behavior and academic performance of students.
- Students' "self-expectations" change according to the labels assigned to them.
- Student performance is highly influenced by self-expectations.
- Stigmatizing labels have a negative impact not only on students' academic performance but their emotions and behavior as well.
- Affirming labels have the positive impact of reinforcing children's belief in their abilities.
- Teacher expectations impact the peer group as well as individual students.

The 1990 "Eye of the Storm" broadcast received high praise. Immediately afterward, school districts and organizations used the film as a training tool. The culture and climate of schools described in chapters 3 and 4 suggest however, that the lessons learned from Elliot's experiment have long since faded.

STIGMATIZING MESSAGES AND SCHOOL DISENGAGEMENT

Messages about the perceived value, abilities, and character of the students and their parents are inherent in the culture and climate of low-performing schools. These messages reinforce the stigma of inferiority, psychologically "keep caste minority students in their place," and as such perpetuate the caste system. As a result of these stigmatizing messages, poor students from caste minority groups disengage from the schooling process early on.

Two dominant messages are received by students, peer groups, and parents: "You are inferior" and "You are not deserving." The pervasiveness and persistence of these messages leads to a great sense of powerlessness on the part of each individual. Students, peer groups, and parents develop their own perceptions of these messages and act accordingly. The model below, adapted from Lee (1991) and expanded by me, describes the relationship between stigmatizing messages and disengagement from the educational process.

INDIVIDUAL STUDENT RESPONSE

For example, a student responded to the question "Why don't you believe that you have a future?" by saying, "When she tells me I ain't nothin', and I ain't goin' to be nothing. I believe her, she is the teacher; she is the one with the power."

Stage 1: Teacher's words and actions demonstrate low expectations; teacher's beliefs about student results in a lack of personal affirmation; student internalizes stereotypes; this leads to a loss of confidence and to lowered self-expectations.
Stage 2: As the result of lowered self-expectations, student fails to develop an academic identity; begins to lack motivation; effort deficit contributes to low academic performance.
Stage 3: Student continues to fail; continued lack of affirmation; student loses hope, begins to feel powerless to change his situation or the teacher's opinion of him; disengages from the educational process; student's failure reinforces teacher's erroneous beliefs about student's ability.

Students who attend schools in stigmatizing environments are constantly bombarded with messages that reinforce stereotypic images of their intellectual ability and moral character. In classrooms, either verbally or nonverbally, the prevailing stereotypes are affirmed. This occurs through nonchallenging, boring coursework, low standards for performance, and messages received from teacher behaviors. The following comments illustrate students' perceptions that a teacher does not expect them to succeed:

- She doesn't call on me.
- She ignores me.
- He ignores my questions.
- He loses my work.
- She doesn't encourage me.
- She tells me that she doesn't expect much from me.

Most significantly, unconscious culturally conditioned beliefs serve as obstacles to the establishment of nurturing relationships with the students most in need of, and positively influenced by, such relationships. Students report that teachers are detached, do not pay attention to them, do not listen to them, do not talk to them, and most importantly disrespect them. This lack of personal affirmation is extremely debilitating to students. The student senses this lack of affirmation and begins to doubt his ability. With the experience of some academic difficulty, persistent lack of affirmation, and relationship failure, the student begins to internalize the stereotypic messages and lowers his self-expectations.

While the student desires to perform well, to gain the recognition of his ability, and affirmation of his worth, the student's low self-expectations lead to his inability to develop an academic identity. Failing to develop an "academic" self, the student now begins to demonstrate an effort deficit in and out of the classroom. As the student experiences more failure, now due to the effort deficit, her lowered self-expectations are reinforced.

The student now feels powerless to demonstrate the competency that will make him feel worthy in the classroom. He continues to receive no affirmation from his teacher; and his continued failure only reinforces the teacher's initial assumptions and beliefs regarding his lack of intellectual ability. He receives no affirmation of his abilities and no support for academic excellence from his peers. As a result, he loses hope and disengages from the schooling process.

PEER-GROUP RESPONSE

Earl was late joining the seventh-grade group of all-male students. They had become accustomed to being called and responding to "Scholar" before their name. As Earl listened to the roll being called, he became increasingly agitated; finally he couldn't take it anymore. "They are lying to you, they aren't no scholars; they can't be scholars," he yelled.

Stage 1: Teacher's words and actions demonstrate low expectations for the peer group; teacher fails to establish affirming relationships with the peer group; the peer group internalizes the stereotypes; peers develop low expectations for the group.

Stage 2: Students observe the failure and treatment of the peer group; they sense disrespect, respond with anger and resistance to teacher, internalize stereotypes associated with the devalued group, and begin to perceive and relate to peers as "stupid" or "bad."

Stage 3: Peer group engages in "expected" behavior, develops an oppositional cultural identity, disengages from the schooling process, engages in behavior that reinforces teacher beliefs about peer group.

It is the observation of the experiences and treatment of peers that has a powerful impact on student attitude and behavior. When students observe students being allowed to sleep in class, to "do nothing," or being told to "do whatever you want to do" or "I have mine," the message they receive is that their education does not matter. Any form of what the peer group regards as disrespect—sarcasm, insensitivity, or public humiliation—sends the message that they are not valued.

The powerlessness experienced by the peer group in stigmatizing environments elicits a response of anger and aggression. The peer group responds to the experience of the lack of affirmation and positive teacher–student relationships through their bonding and resistance to dictates from teachers and administrators. It is also the peer group, through their observation of the "failures" of their peers, that internalizes the stereotypes of intellectual inferiority. Very much aware of the messages of inferiority that they are receiving, as they observe their peers struggling and failing, they begin to develop low expectations for the capacity of their peers as well as themselves.

The oppositional identity exhibited by many males, especially in caste minority groups, is influenced by their internalization of the low expectations held of them by teachers and administrators. As a result of the lowered peer expectations, they fail to develop a group academic identity and demonstrate a group effort deficit. They also demonstrate group resistance to the low expectations and "disrespect" they perceive from the teacher by refusing to work, playing around, talking, failing to bring necessary materials to class, failing to participate in class, and so on.

While the oppositional identity and accusations of "acting white" have been widely discussed, little attention has been paid to the mimicking of low expectations, the putting down and demeaning of peers who perform poorly in the classroom. Ferguson (2001) contends that the diminished motivation of African American males to identify themselves as scholars is a consequence of the inhospitable culture of school rather than the consequences of peer pressure. Ferguson suggests that school practices, cultural differences, and underlying messages actually set African American boys up for school failure. Like Earl, they arrive at a point of refusing to believe that students who look like themselves are capable of academic achievement.

PARENT RESPONSE

Comment from parent:"Those teachers don't care about our kids."

Stage 1: Through words and actions, the parent receives messages that indicate low expectations for her child; these messages make her recall her own negative school experience; she begins to distrust the administrators and teachers to do what is best for her child.

Stage 2: The parent feels powerless to assist her child in having a more successful educational outcome than she experienced; she lowers her expectations for her child's success.

Stage 3: The parent's sense of powerlessness causes her to fail to engage or to disengage from involvement in her child's schooling process.

A parent's prior school experience is a major factor that will contribute to his or her sense of powerlessness as it relates to his or her child's school experience. The level of anger and distrust felt by parents of caste minority children is influenced by their prior school experience. If the parent attended a post-*Brown* segregated school or had a negative school experience, his or her sense of powerlessness to contribute or control his or her child's educational outcome will be greater.

As the parent senses or recognizes familiar aspects of the stigmatizing environment, her distrust of the school and lack of belief in the educational process will grow. It is this sense of familiarity with the stigmatizing environment that will lead the parent to lose hope that the schooling of her child will be more positive and beneficial than her own.

As the parent receives the messages related to the undervaluing of her child and low expectations for her child's academic ability, she herself begins to lower her expectations for her child's success in the school setting. Any and every negative experience with the school involving her child will only confirm her initial reservations. She will finally lose faith in the school and disengage to a level of only doing what is legally or officially required. Her sense of powerlessness will most likely be interpreted as not caring about the education of her child.

Academic failure can pretty much be guaranteed for students who attend school in stigmatizing environments. The stigmatizing messages, the pervasive sense of powerlessness, and the lowering of individual, peer group, and parent expectations for academic success lead to unsuccessful educational outcomes for students from caste minority groups. Unless the cycle is broken, most poor minority children attending post-*Brown* segregated schools will remain trapped in the underclass.

One of the major reasons that issues related to the stigmatizing aspects of school environments are not addressed is the illusion that after *Brown* the educational system is now color-blind. While the ideology that created segregated schools in the pre-*Brown* era is very much alive and well, as evidenced in chapter 3, the illusion of a color-blind educational system prevents us from recognizing and acknowledging the damaging impact of the stigmatization to which students attending post-*Brown* segregated schools are subjected.

Finally, an early theory devised by Sue (1981) provides some insights that may be helpful in understanding the negative impact of color-blind education upon poor minority children and especially the lack of any mechanism by which to have their issues in stigmatizing environments addressed. Sue (1981) presents a conceptual model that identifies factors considered to be important in understanding two psychological orientations: locus of control and locus of responsibility.

LOCUS OF CONTROL

The locus of control has internal and external dimensions. Internal control is related to an individual's beliefs that reinforcements are contingent upon their own actions; external control focuses on people's beliefs that reinforcing events occur independently of their actions (i.e., chance and fate).

Members of ethnic minority groups and those of lower socioeconomic groups score significantly higher on the external end of the continuum. A sense of powerlessness or the expectancy that one's behavior cannot determine the outcomes one seeks contributes to the external focus of control. According to Sue (1981), focusing on external forces may in fact be motivationally healthy if this belief results from assessing one's chances for success against systematic obstacles.

LOCUS OF RESPONSIBILITY

Locus of responsibility measures the degree of responsibility or blame placed upon the individual or system for individual outcomes. The person-centered orientation (IR) holds that an individual's success or failure is attributable to the individual's skills, ability, effort, and personal adequacies or the lack thereof. Situation-centered blame or blame of the system (ER) views the socioeconomic environment as more potent than the individual. Success or failure is thought to depend on the system and not necessarily on the individual.

Members of minority groups typically view factors such as institutional racism as determinants of their success or failure in the society. Individuals who espouse system blame are more apt to blame environmental forces rather than personal inadequacies as factors that block the achievement of their goals.

The orientation of students in pre-*Brown* segregated schools tended to be that of internal control (IC) and system blame (ER). Students were prodded to work hard, and they understood that their efforts and actions (even having to work twice as hard) were necessary for success. The culture and climates of good black segregated schools, especially the nurturing personal relationships, enabled the students to develop this sense of internal control.

However, even while accepting responsibility for their success, students were made aware of and recognized that societal factors threatened the outcomes for which they strove. This system-blame orientation created a collective philosophy of education—a mechanism for coping with the barriers the group faced.

Color-blind education in post-*Brown* segregated schools reinforces the traditional mainstream internal control (IC), internal responsibility (IR) orientation while ignoring the obstacles related to race and class that students attending these schools face. Poor minority students and/or their parents are held solely responsible for the students' success or failure in the face of stereotypical images, low expectations, and in many cases hostile environments. The indirect and subtle forms of stigmatization experienced by students in post-*Brown* segregated schools are much more destructive in many ways than the overt discrimination for which pre-*Brown* segregated schools prepared black students.

Unfortunately, the response of students in stigmatizing environments to their continued academic failure is intrapunitive; they internalize the stereotype of inferiority and begin to blame themselves for their failure. They come to believe that in the *school setting*, something is lacking in them; as a result, they fail to develop an academic identity or confidence in their abilities.

However, in stigmatizing environments, an external control (EC) is the most realistic response. Both the experience and the pain of those experiences are denied; as a result, students remain confused, frustrated, and angry, knowing intuitively that they are perceived and treated differently. According to Sue (1981), constant and prolonged failure or the inability to attain goals leads to symptoms of self-blame, such as depression, guilt, and feelings of inadequacy.

This self-blame is exemplified in the lowered self-expectations, effort deficit, and ultimate disengagement from the schooling process by students from caste minority groups. In addition, because the prevailing orientation of the "postracial" era is one of individual responsibility (IR) for success or failure in the society, students are not provided with a mechanism or the tools to confront or challenge the inequities still faced by caste minorities in this society. A focus on education only for individual gain has overshadowed the collective purpose of education, which was crucial for the success of caste minority groups in the pre-*Brown* era.

The work of Ogbu, international studies, and the Elliot experiment all give testimony to the differential educational experiences of students from caste minority groups and the debilitating impact of stigmatization. The illusion of color-blind education prevents us from seriously examining the school's responsibility to change the structure of education for these students and to take responsibility for their undereducation. The model proposed by Sue suggests the pitfalls of holding students in stigmatizing environments to the same standards of achievement as those for students who are free from these barriers.

This is in no way intended to mean lowering of standards for poor minority students; instead, it is meant to suggest that cultures and climates of schools attended by these students be totally restructured with the sociopolitical reality of our schools in mind. The reality is a "full-circle" return to segregated schools in the post-*Brown* era. Within the context of post-*Brown* segregated schools, how can the education of poor minority students be restructured so that it meets their needs in a society that is not yet postracial?

In the next chapter, the keys to the success of "good" historically black segregated schools is discussed. These schools were able to assist students in developing an internal locus of control while at the same time preparing them to realistically face the challenges imposed by segregation and discrimination. In addition, these schools, under the worst of conditions, managed to graduate legions of well-educated individuals and to produce leaders. There is much that we can learn from pre-*Brown* segregated schools about how to effectively teach poor children from caste minority groups.

Part III

IS EDUCATIONAL EQUITY POSSIBLE?

6

Lessons from Historically Black Segregated Schools

WE BECAME INVISIBLE

In the section below, I describe a return to the all-black high school I had previously attended.

A few years ago, I decided to visit my old, formerly all-black high school. The school, located in an all-black neighborhood, was closed during the initial stages of desegregation but has since reopened as a celebrated magnet school of the arts. I was valedictorian of my class and a plaque listing the valedictorians from each school year was prominently displayed in the foyer. When I visited, to my surprise and disappointment, not only was the plaque missing but so were the cases containing sports memorabilia. All evidence of this once being an all-black school was erased; since desegregation, my once-proud all-black school had become invisible.

I proceeded to find the principal to discuss the missing memorabilia. She was courteous and apologetic. She particularly expressed concern about the missing sports trophies. To her understanding, our school had once been "a sports powerhouse." I corrected her: "We had been an academic powerhouse." At the time of my attendance, academic excellence was a priority. The principal's comments were indicative of long-held and erroneous beliefs about all-black schools—that they were populated by students with superior athletic ability but inferior intellect.

The image of historically black segregated schools that lingers in the national mind is one of inferiority: dilapidated facilities crowded with poor, ignorant, ill-behaved children taught by barely literate teachers. It is this image or "national memory," according to Walker (1996), that dominates the thinking related to the segregated schooling of black children.

This memory, which focuses primarily on the inferior education received by black children in historically black segregated schools, has its roots in the ideology of black intellectual inferiority. The ideology of black intellectual inferiority was used to justify the denial of equal funding to black schools, the double taxation of blacks, and ultimately as a tool to preserve and reinforce the racial caste system in the South.

This ideology served another significant purpose during the desegregation process. It contributed to the closing and downgrading of historically black schools, the massive layoffs of black teachers, and the demotion of black administrators. According to Dempsey and Noblit (1996), black schools were stigmatized as undesirable educational settings as a result of the political process surrounding desegregation.

The image of historically black segregated schools as second-rate, filled with intellectually inferior students, and taught by inadequately prepared teachers is mythical. This image also belies the fact that blacks resisted and circumvented the caste education designed for them and that black children were effectively educated prior to attending school with whites. Walker (1996) suggests that the uniform image of black segregated schools as being without merit should be called into question.

According to Fairclough (2007), histories of all-black schools indicate that these segregated black high schools were centers of scholarly excellence. Many of these institutions with both long histories and proud traditions had been successful institutions under segregation. In fact, a few were considered to be as academically successful as the best white schools.

Jones (1981) suggests that there has been little attention paid by social science researchers to effective black public schools and the impact that these schools can have on poor black students. Positive views of these schools are outnumbered by negative views that "exude an attitude" of hopelessness. In a study of all-black Dunbar High School in Little Rock, Arkansas, Jones (1981) found characteristics that promoted successful learning in spite of the segregated system, and Morris and Morris (2002) suggest that African American communities provided a "good education" for their children long before the 1954 *Brown* decision.

It would, of course, be naïve to assume that all historically black segregated schools were good schools or that all teachers and administrators were exemplary. Colorism and classism were negative elements known to exist in historically segregated black schools (Morris & Morris, 2002). Historically black schools from the Jim Crow era cannot be romanticized. There is little to doubt about the neglect and inferior aspects of historically black segregated schools during the era of Jim Crow.

Black education was consistently underfunded, while black parents suffered "double taxation": they paid taxes for public schools that were all diverted to white schools and supported black schools through their meager earnings and labor. Most structures were dilapidated or inadequate at best—some without adequate heat or even inside restrooms for students. Black schools lacked libraries, auditoriums, and even cafeterias.

Students were issued secondhand books and were not provided the necessary materials. Teachers taught multiple grades in overcrowded classrooms. Teachers who were paid at rates significantly lower than those of their white counterparts used their own funds to buy needed supplies for the classroom. Fortunately, because of the trust and positive relationships that existed between parents, the community, and the schools, financial and material support was provided when necessary.

By the same token, historically black segregated schools cannot be mythologized as bastions of intellectual inferiority, filled with ignorant students and barely literate teachers. Historically black segregated schools graduated legions of students who became responsible and productive citizens as well as a cadre of well-educated blacks who became leaders of the movement to desegregate public schools. The characteristics of the schools described in this chapter are those of good black schools—schools that were successful in effectively educating students who were racially stigmatized.

Dempsey and Noblit (1996) assert that "it is clear that we did not understand what those [segregated] schools provided for African American children." According to Walker (1996), evidence suggests that in spite of the poor facilities and funding, the environment of segregated schools had affective traits, institutional policies, and community support that enabled black children to learn. It was this focus on the affective domain that was the crucial element in the successful schooling of black children during the era of Jim Crow.

The culture, climate, and curriculum—all crucial to the context of historically black segregated schooling—enabled black students to face and adapt to a future marred by the bleakness of Jim Crow laws and customs. These elements made the difference between merely teaching subject matter and inspiring students to lives of purpose and service to the community.

The school culture was informed by deeply held beliefs about the purpose of education in the lives of black children, their innate potential, the role of teachers, and the collective responsibility of teachers and administrators. The school climate, often described as being like a "family," was characterized by nurturing teacher–student relationships. An "expansive" curriculum provided space for discovering gifts and talents and the development of leadership skills. Most significantly, "interventions" were in place that helped black children to transcend the stigma imposed by caste membership.

A PHILOSOPHY OF EDUCATION

The educational experience of students attending historically black segregated schools was shaped by a deeply felt belief that education was the only route by which students and the community "could advance as a race" (Cecelski, 1994). This philosophy of education, forged in slavery and passed on throughout history, emphasized education for freedom, racial uplift, citizenship, and leadership (Perry, Steele, and Hilliard, 2003).

Acquiring an education was viewed as a tool of empowerment—a means of gaining equality in society. It was this overarching *collective orientation* of black education that gave schooling and achievement a higher purpose. The benefits of an education were to be shared and utilized for the benefit of the collective—the race. This collective meaning of the value of education meant that one did not use one's education "to get out" but rather "to give back" and that this purpose could not be dislodged even in the face of discrimination and lack of commensurate employment opportunities.

Teachers and administrators themselves understood the realities of caste minority membership and prepared students to adapt to this social reality, albeit not in the ways that white school officials intended. Black educators sabotaged and circumvented efforts to provide a "special" or caste education that trained black children for menial jobs and subservience.

Historically black segregated schools had mechanisms and interventions, known as the hidden curriculum (Foster, 1997), in place to address social stigmatization and provide tools to empower black students despite the world of second-class citizenship that they would enter. The social reality, in which race was central, gave direction to the policies and practices of historically black segregated schools.

With this understanding of the sociopolitical reality, historically black segregated schools met the unique affective needs of black students. While the larger society sent deprecating messages about the Negro's value and status, the school provided countermessages (Walker, 1996).

In the school setting, stereotypes were refuted. New identities were shaped and alternative realities were created based upon the attributes that had enabled blacks to survive and thrive through the most difficult of times. It was the direct intervention to nullify the larger society's stigmatization that was the greatest achievement of historically black segregated schools. When black students entered the schoolroom, their humanity was affirmed, their heritage celebrated, and their dignity restored.

THE CULTURE OF HISTORICALLY BLACK SEGREGATED SCHOOLS

The culture that existed in pre-*Brown* segregated schools was undergirded by a set of core beliefs related to the capacity of black students and beliefs about the role and responsibility of those who taught them. This belief system, which influenced personal philosophies and teaching practices, was a crucial element related to the achievement of black children in historically black segregated schools. This belief system has been demonstrated in the research of Walker (1996), Jones (1981), Foster (1997), and Dempsey and Noblit (1996); that research is drawn upon in the following sections.

BELIEFS ABOUT STUDENTS

The beliefs held about black students who attended historically black segregated schools were the antithesis of the beliefs of black intellectual and cultural inferiority held by the larger society. These beliefs were not only held but demonstrated daily through the words and actions of teachers and administrators. Belief in the capacity of students shaped an educational environment that nurtured, encouraged, and inspired high academic achievement. In historically black segregated schools, the following core beliefs were held about students:

- Students had unlimited potential. Because teachers refuted the ideology of black intellectual inferiority, they placed no limits on a student's capacity. Students were not defined or limited by their family configuration or living conditions. Students were constantly encouraged to dream and to be all that they could be.
- All children could learn and succeed. Teachers understood that there would be individual differences, strengths and weaknesses, but they believed that each child possessed some gift or talent that could be discovered and developed.
- Any child could rise above his or her current life condition. Teachers believed that one's current life situation did not necessarily determine one's future condition. With enough care and attention from the teacher, a child's life could be changed.

These beliefs in the capacity of students were demonstrated through high expectations held for student performance. This meant never giving up on students and demanding that they work up to and beyond what they, the students, perceived their abilities to be.

BELIEFS ABOUT TEACHER ROLE AND RESPONSIBILITY

Teaching was perceived to be "a high and worthy calling" (Fairclough, 2007). Teaching was viewed as a "mission" rather than simply a job. Because education was viewed as a means to uplift the race, teachers had a personal stake in being sure that each student reached his or her full potential. Teachers felt that by successfully engaging a student in learning, they contributed to the community and to racial uplift (Walker, 1996). Fairclough (2007) suggests that segregation fostered a special sense of commitment whereby black teachers identified with their schools.

The teacher's role consisted of many aspects; role model, motivator, presenter, goader, and counselor. The teacher was considered to be the "most essential part of the educational process" (Jones, 1981). Teachers were also expected to be role models in the community, to participate in community events, to demonstrate exemplary behavior, and even to dress properly.

Again, the seminal work of Walker (1996), Foster (1997), Jones (1981) and Dempsey and Noblit (1996) provides insights into the belief systems of black teachers in historically black segregated schools. The core beliefs held by teachers about their role and responsibility were as follows:

- Teachers were responsible for student achievement. A student's failure was a teacher's failure. It was the duty of the teacher to determine what obstacles may be interfering with student mastery of material. Teachers recognized the influence of personal and family problems that the student may be experiencing; however, the student and/or his family was never considered the sole reason for poor academic performance. Teachers looked internally when students repeatedly failed to grasp material. When students did not learn, teachers asked " Did I teach?"
- It was the responsibility of teachers to keep students engaged. They believed that the manner in which material was presented could be the cause of poor student performance; therefore they sought better ways to present material as well as to give their attention to individual students. The teacher assumed responsibility for helping to motivate students to learn.
- Teaching was more than delivering subject matter. The mantra of former teachers from the era of historically black segregated schools is that you must "teach the whole child." These teachers believed that you "could not separate the teaching from the taught." Teachers were committed to the development of the whole child and to molding individuals who could successfully participate in the struggle for equality.
- Teachers were obliged to believe in a child and his or her ability until the child was able to believe in himself or herself. This belief was demonstrated by holding the highest of expectations for students and never giving up on them. Once teachers demonstrated their trust in a child's ability, the student came to trust himself and to take risks that otherwise he would not have. Demonstrating belief in a student also built the kind of trust that created a positive teacher–student relationship.

Narratives from historically black schools provided descriptions of the characteristics of a good teacher:

- The basis of good teaching was felt to be concern and caring for a child no matter who he or she was (Walker, 1996). Good teachers can often be heard to say, "A child doesn't care what you know until he knows that you care."
- Good teachers took students from where they were and helped them to grow from there (Walker, 1996).
- Good teachers motivated and inspired students; they encouraged students to want to learn. Good teaching produced students with disciplined minds who did not simply regurgitate information but were able to question, locate information, evaluate evidence, make reasoned judgments, and solve problems (Jones, 1981).

Holding these core beliefs about the potential of students and about their roles and responsibilities was crucial to the effective teaching of students who were otherwise stigmatized.

Because they were not victimized by erroneous beliefs and false assumptions about the capacity of their students, teachers believed in their own efficacy and were empowered to guide students to achievement despite the inequities in funding and resources that they experienced.

THE CLIMATE OF HISTORICALLY BLACK SEGREGATED SCHOOLS

The school climate or educational environment is an outward expression and demonstration of the belief system espoused by teachers and administrators. That belief system influences policies, teaching practices, and specific teaching behaviors, such as relationship building.

BOOKER HIGH SCHOOL

Booker High School was all about business. Professor Rogers ("Fess") was a no-nonsense principal. There was no playing around, only attending to the task at hand. Students understood that they were being educated for a higher purpose. Teachers were warm, attentive, and interested in students as individuals. The one thing that teachers did not allow was for students to stray from the path of achievement; there were no excuses for failure. Because of the care, trust, support, and investment of teachers, students felt that they had a responsibility to learn all that they could. Achievement meant making parents, teachers, and the community proud.

The climate of a good historically black segregated school was purposeful, supportive, nurturing, and strict. There was a collective sense of responsibility and commitment to student success. High expectations were held for students and high standards were the norm. The formal and informal curriculum promoted student empowerment, and the informal curriculum in particular was significant in the development of the "whole person." Most importantly, according to Irvine and Irvine (1983), the segregated black school was an educational institution that addressed the deeper psychological and sociological needs of students.

This affective focus was implemented in three major ways: caring relationships, mechanisms to empower students and develop leadership skills, and direct interventions designed to address issues related to race and caste minority status.

CARING RELATIONSHIPS

The characteristic of the historically black segregated schools most often mentioned by students who attended them was the sense of "family" that prevailed. The feeling of connection was fostered by the nurturing relationships established by teachers with students. It was this "practice of caring" that has been discussed by historians of historically black segregated schools (Walker, 1996; Foster, 1997; Dempsey & Noblit, 1997; Cecelski, 1994; Jones, 1981).

The teacher–student relationship was felt to be the most crucial element facilitating the achievement of students who attended these schools. Walker (1996) describes interpersonal caring as the "direct attention given to meet the psychological, sociological, and academic needs of another individual or individuals." Caring relationships were the hallmark of good historically black segregated schools.

In good historically black segregated schools, the task of teaching students was not inconsistent with the development of caring relationships with students. According to Dempsey and Noblit (1997), caring meant nurturing students as well as providing valuable information. Three aspects of caring relationships were (1) personal attention, (2) probing, and (3) pushing.

- *Personal attention*: Teachers were interested in students as individuals; they were available to students. This personal attention meant respecting individual differences and helping students to discover and develop unique gifts and talents; providing guidance related to life goals; and sometimes even giving material or financial assistance. By the same token, personal attention meant holding students to high standards—no excuses.

- *Probing*: was used to determine the cause of problematic behavior. When students experienced problems in class, seemed unmotivated or disengaged, teachers sought to find the source of the problem. It was through a trusting relationship between teacher and student that teachers were able to diagnose and eliminate obstacles to student achievement.
- *Pushing*: One of the most often referred to interventions used by black teachers to "raise the bar" and set higher standards for their students was the act of pushing. Pushing a student to do more or better was a significant demonstration of teacher caring and belief in a student's ability.

Pushing might be defined as the demand that a student perform at a higher level than the student thought he or she was capable of. Even when students resisted and spoke of their teachers as being mean or difficult, their faces expressed delight in knowing that the teacher cared enough to push them to higher levels of achievement.

AN EXAMPLE OF PUSHING

It was either in seventh or eight grade when students in Mrs. Dailey's English class were required to learn and recite poems (to "stand and deliver"). Mrs. Dailey selected a list of classic poems from which students could choose. I, like many of the other students, chose to recite "The House by the Side of the Road." Mrs. Dailey quietly but firmly informed me that "you can do better" and assigned instead "The Wreck of the Hesperus."

Individual students could be pushed by a teacher who felt that they could do better, or an entire class could be expected to perform outside of its comfort zone. Again in Mrs. Dailey's English class, junior and senior students were expected to write essays to compete in countywide essay contests (which, surprisingly, black students were allowed to enter). Students had no choice; though not part of the requirements of the formal curriculum, students were pushed to write to win. Because of the pushing that I received, I won two of those contests.

THE SALIENCY OF RACE

Meeting the affective needs of students resulting from stigmatizing caste status was one of the most significant functions of teachers in historically black segregated schools. Lessons in racial pride and self-respect were woven into the curriculum. Being able to instill a sense of black identity and dignity was considered essential to a teacher's success (Baker, 2006; Cecelski, 1994). Persisting in the face of racism, struggling for equality, developing their talents to be used in service to the community, and understanding that they, the students, were "somebody" were also crucial lessons taught in historically black segregated schools.

According to Perry and colleagues (2003), historically black segregated schools were intentionally organized in opposition to the ideology of black intellectual inferiority. Institutional practices as well as expected behaviors and outcomes were designed to counter the ideology of black intellectual inferiority. In addition, the teachers and administrators of historically black segregated schools promoted curricular, behavioral, and ritualistic practices designed to counter the status of blacks as a racial caste group.

CRITICAL DIALOGUES

"Critical dialogues" were utilized to refute the stereotypes of blacks held by the larger society and to affirm their worth. Foster (1990) describes critical dialogues as necessary to engage students in their own learning. These dialogues included personal values, collective power, and the political consequences of choosing academic achievement.

Critical dialogues were related to:

- The value of education. Through formal and informal dialogues, teachers helped students to understand that education was their only hope for a better life. Young blacks had only two options: to get an education or expect to work in menial labor. Blacks could not, like whites, expect to leave school and become tellers in the banks, clerks in stores, or secretaries in offices; the only options were domestic work for females and manual labor for males.
- Emphasis on hard work and the reality of the competition they faced. It was made clear to students that simply becoming educated was not enough. A common message that black students in historically black segregated schools received was that "You will have to be twice as good [as a white student] to succeed." Students were admonished not to waste their time, because as blacks they would need all of the preparation that they could get in order to face a difficult reality.
- Counternarratives (Perry, 2003; Walker, 1996). Black students, like their parents, received messages from the larger society about their assumed inferiority. Segregation was meant to reinforce this sense of otherness and of being less than whites. A narrative designed to coun-

ter that of African American intellectual inferiority was one of African Americans as a literate and achieving people. These counternarratives were passed on in historically black segregated schools.

Counternarratives included stories about the African American struggle for literacy, the purpose of literacy, and the liberating and empowering potential of literacy. These counternarratives played a critical role in creating an achievement identity among black students and in helping them to develop those attitudes and behaviors essential for academic success. In these dialogues, teachers countered society's negative messages.

EXTRACURRICULAR ACTIVITIES

In historically black segregated schools, what are commonly regarded as extracurricular activities were ritualized and formalized into the school's curriculum. The very nature and role of these segregated schools required that attention be given to more than the state-mandated formal curriculum. In "advancing the race," the mission of historically black segregated schools required the development of leaders. Morris and Morris (2002) suggest that developing the leadership skills of school-age children was a "critical strategy" for uplifting the race.

Extracurricular activities were also an integral part of the school experience of students in historically black segregated schools because of the goal of developing the whole person. According to Morris and Morris (2002), many of the activities considered part of after-school programs in schools today were integrated into the school day in the black segregated school. In addition to leadership skills, these activities contributed to the positive development of students' academic, social, and lifelong leisure skills.

Histories from pre-*Brown* black segregated schools indicate that there was an emphasis on the cultural value of the oral tradition. From the earliest grades, students were expected to participate in extracurricular activities, to learn to speak, and to perform before audiences. These school programs allowed students to develop confidence, share special talents, and have a sense of being important members of the school community. From elementary through secondary school, students were given the opportunity to:

- Discover, develop, and express a variety of gifts and talents
- Explore and cultivate new interests and to broaden their horizons
- Build confidence and enhance self-esteem
- Practice collectivistic values—unity, cooperation, and working toward a common goal
- Most importantly, they were encouraged to develop leadership skills.

CHAPEL

Chapel was a significant aspect of the informal curriculum of every historically black segregated school. It was a weekly ritual of devotion, inspiration,
and instruction. That hour, usually on a Friday morning, gave students
the opportunity to be inspired, learn about their history, appreciate their
heritage, discover their gifts and talents, and develop leadership skills. Most
students who attended a historically black segregated school have fond
memories of chapel.

Especially at the secondary level, chapel gave students the opportunity
to plan, organize, and present a student-led program. Here students could
apply the knowledge gained from textbooks and the classroom. It was in
chapel that public speaking skills were honed and leadership skills developed. These were not hours spent in talent shows, singing and dancing, but
rather time spent in gaining the knowledge and practicing the skills that
students would need as future leaders.

Chapel was an especially important venue for the teaching of black history. Students were exposed to the literature and poetry of black Americans and learned to appreciate it. They learned about the contributions of
important personalities. Most students who attended a historically black
segregated school will remember standing and singing "Lift Every Voice and
Sing," the Negro national anthem, at the beginning of each chapel meeting.

THE CURRICULUM

Many secondary schools established for blacks were based upon the
Hampton-Tuskegee model, which emphasized vocational and mechanical
training. There was general opposition among southern school officials to
academic training or to liberal education for blacks. As mentioned earlier,
the goal of education for blacks was simply to provide the rudimentary
skills that would be useful to white employers while not providing an education that would make blacks competitive in the workplace or encourage
blacks to forget their own place in southern society.

Black teachers and administrators circumvented this caste education and
provided a liberal and college preparatory education that included courses
in English Grammar, English Literature, History, Biology, Chemistry, Physics, Algebra I and II, Geometry, Trigonometry, and even, in some cases,
foreign languages. While the state may have mandated a curriculum that
included Agriculture and Home Economics, an expansive rather than restrictive curriculum, as prescribed by white officials, was implemented in
good historically black segregated schools.

One teacher interviewed by Foster (1997), who had taught in a previously all-black school, described black teachers as "subversive." She suggested that teachers expanded the curriculum in ways not sanctioned by the school board; what they taught about race was not in textbooks.

This expansive curriculum was a direct reflection of the belief in students' abilities and commitment to the larger purpose of educating people who would be prepared to lead the race. This expansive curriculum made it possible for students like me to be fully prepared to attend college without experiencing academic problems and to study successfully in and graduate from predominately white institutions.

Foster (1997) suggests that we look at the past through "new eyes" in order to determine what we might learn about how to address current issues in educating African American children. What we can learn most from historically black segregated schools is the critical importance of addressing the affective domain in educating these students. Any serious attempts at reform for poor minority students must include in their design mechanisms and interventions to address the impact of caste minority membership.

According to Dempsey and Noblit (1996), understanding how historically black segregated schools created a context of caring may teach us not only about what African American children need to be successful but also about what all children need. Finally, Walker (1996) suggests that "African American teachers and principals who taught students in oppressive circumstances may have much to teach as they remind current educators of the importance of building self-esteem, of placing high expectations, and of being willing to provide individual attention to students."

How specifically did the belief system and educational environment of historically black segregated schools impact student achievement?

- Students felt valued and developed a sense of their own worth.
- Students developed confidence in their academic abilities.
- Students felt connected to and a part of the school community.
- Students had positive feelings about and were engaged in the schooling process.
- Students placed a high value on education.
- Students perceived themselves as learners and aspired to high academic achievement.
- Students felt a responsibility to not disappoint those who had encouraged and supported their learning.
- Students believed they possessed the attitudes and skills which would enable them to face and overcome the obstacles they would face as a result of Jim Crow.

What can be learned from historically segregated black schools about how to effectively educate students from caste minority groups?

- Teachers have tremendous power to affect positive educational outcomes.
- The belief systems of teachers and their faith in the ability of students and their own efficacy will influence teaching practices and the quality of their relationships with students.
- The quality of the teacher–student relationship will in large measure influence student motivation and achievement.
- A sense of collective responsibility on the part of teachers and administrators must prevail in the school setting.
- It is critical to address the affective (psychological and sociological) needs of students.
- The formal curriculum must be expansive and the informal curriculum must be an integral part of the schooling process.
- Issues of race and class must be addressed through direct intervention.

The educational reality today is that there has been a return to a segregated public school system. Schools attended by a majority of poor black and brown students are those in which students are both stigmatized and undereducated. It does not appear that poverty or racism will be eliminated in this society in the near future. Through serious reform, however, schools can take steps to ensure that children from stigmatized groups receive the "special" education that is required to change their life conditions and improve their life chances.

In chapter 7, socially responsive pedagogy is introduced as a mechanism for replicating some of the important lessons learned from historically black segregated schools, focusing on ways to effectively educate students from caste minority groups.

7

Socially Responsive Pedagogy

If there must be a return to segregated schools, let them be good ones; at the least, let them not be worse than the previous ones.

School segregation has come full circle from pre-*Brown* to post-*Brown* segregated schools. This new segregation, like the Jim Crow segregation that preceded it, denies equal educational opportunity to students from caste minority groups. The caste education designed by southern school officials was intended to thwart the educational, economic, social, and political aspirations of African Americans. As described in chapter 6, within the broader context of the segregated system, African American teachers and administrators in many historically black segregated schools created an alternative educational context that empowered African American students who were stigmatized in the larger society.

Today, black and brown children are again relegated to schools segregated by race and class. In this new segregation, students attempt to learn in often less than adequate facilities, with few resources and low expectations. They are forced into an oppressive testing cycle that further limits their educational experience. In the present context of segregated schools, how can schooling be provided that meets the academic and social needs of poor minority students? How can an alternative to the school environments in which these students are further stigmatized and disempowered be designed? How can their further undereducation be prevented? As for those in the pre-*Brown* era of segregated schools, the only hope for these students is human capital—the courage of teachers and administrators who care enough about these students to create an alternative educational context for them. First and foremost, however, poor students from minority groups *should not* be required to leave the public school system in order to receive a quality education. It was, in fact, free public education that many of their ancestors struggled to establish, to maintain during the Jim Crow era, and to seek equal access to during the desegregation period.

MOVING FROM A STIGMATIZING TO AN AFFIRMING EDUCATIONAL ENVIRONMENT

An administrative staff and faculty can *choose* to provide a quality education for the poor minority students that attend a low-performing school. They can make a conscious decision to change the school culture and climate despite the high-stakes testing context in which schools for poor minority students now currently operate. Like their predecessors in historically black segregated schools, if they have the *will* to do so, they can circumvent the current system which condemns poor minority children to a caste education and perpetual caste minority membership.

The goal of any such action taken by an administrative staff and faculty will be to change the structure of the educational process so that the school recognizes, accepts, and responds to the sociopolitical reality of its students. This means that the quality of the educational environment and experience of students attending the school must change, as well as the relationships with parents and the community. In order for this to occur, changes must occur in the:

- Philosophy of educating the student population
- Belief system that forms the school culture
- Internal and external image of the school
- School curriculum, with a focus on affective education
- Acceptance by the faculty and staff of *collective responsibility* for both the success and failure of students to achieve in the school

In order to change the structure and context of schooling for students, the administrative staff and faculty must be willing to engage a pedagogy that is not based upon deficit thinking and rooted in the ideology of inferiority. *Socially responsive pedagogy* is offered as an alternative to the conventional and ineffective approaches that have failed to produce improved outcomes for students from poor minority groups.

SOCIALLY RESPONSIVE PEDAGOGY

Socially responsive pedagogy (SRP) is based on the premise that school environments must support educational outcomes; that pedagogy must be informed by the actual experiences of students; and that affirming, nurturing environments with high expectations can produce high academic achievers no matter the students' race or social class. SRP responds to the life experiences of poor students from caste minority groups and the sociopolitical context in which they are schooled.

This approach directly addresses the obstacles imposed by race and caste stigmatization in the larger society and in the school setting. SRP provides a framework for transforming the culture and climate of "low-performing" schools—those in which poor students from caste minority groups are chronically undereducated.

SRP emphasizes that, for improved educational outcomes, belief system change must occur at both the institutional level and within students. SRP operates to create learning environments in which students can develop the beliefs, attitudes, and skills necessary to change their life conditions and to help them become agents of change in their communities. SRP involves direct affective interventions that serve as a prerequisite and support for learning.

SRP draws upon the work of Paulo Freire's (Del Pilar et al., 1998) *re-orientation of the curriculum* model. Freire asserts that the curriculum must be based on the realities of student lives. It is also grounded in cognitive behavioral theory, which recognizes that change in belief systems is integral to structural changes in individual or institutional behaviors. In this case, SRP requires changes in those institutional belief systems that are based on stereotypical images of the poor and minorities, which are informed by the ideology of inferiority, and which ultimately result in the creation of stigmatizing school environments.

SRP acknowledges the sociopolitical context in which schooling takes place. It recognizes that the social milieu of our schools—especially those segregated by race and class—replicates that of the larger society, and that if there truly is a desire to lift students from their low-caste status, major structural changes must take place in post-*Brown* segregated schools. To accomplish this task, the SRP model consists of four phases (textbox 7.1) that target the school's culture and climate and involve teachers/administrators, students, and families.

Steps such as imposing common standards, providing massive doses of money, restructuring school staffs, firing teachers, and closing schools will not correct the chronic undereducation of poor minority students. Unless the sociopolitical context in which these students are schooled is transformed, no improvement or meaningful change in educational outcomes will occur. Reform must begin with institutional change, and such change must occur in the very core philosophies and belief systems that undergird the education of these students.

Much of this book is devoted to identifying areas that are deficient in terms of teacher beliefs and attitudes; in their defense, however, it must be

---

Textbox 7.1.   Socially Responsive Pedagogy

Phase I: Restructuring the School Culture (Institutional Change)

- Staff development
- Redefinition of the problem
- Philosophy of education

Phase II: Reengagement of Family and Community

- Building of trust
- Redefining roles

Phase III: Reconstructing the School Image

- Collaboration of faculty/staff/students/families/community

Phase IV: Restructuring the School Climate

- Affective domain
- Cognitive domain

---

said that the majority of teachers and administrators who find themselves responsible for schooling poor minority students are grossly ill prepared to do so. They lack awareness of the sociopolitical context in which they are schooling these students; they lack (accurate) knowledge of the educational and affective needs of these students resulting from low-caste membership; and they lack the skills necessary to assist students in using education as a tool for life change.

Teachers in these segregated schools are stressed and frustrated; they-doubt their own efficacy and are robbed of their power as teachers by personal and institutional beliefs based upon the ideology of inferiority. Teachers have not been required to engage in the type of critical reflection or cognitive restructuring process (Bireda, 2010) that will develop in them both the attitudes and attributes to be effective teachers for this group of students. As a result, criteria for evaluating the performance of teachers have not included a demonstration of positive beliefs in or high expectancy for their students. Teachers are evaluated by student performance on tasks that they themselves are doubtful that their students can achieve.

From 1965 to 1975, there was a concerted effort to provide sensitivity training to teachers. Over the next twenty years, however, efforts waned and sensitivity training was more a reactive response to complaints and Office of Civil Rights (OCR) mandates than a proactive one. By the 1990s, there was a total change of focus, and by the time No Child Left Behind became law, schools were asked to change the "soft bigotry of low expectations"—but in a climate of "color-blind" education that prohibited addressing the issue of race.

PHASE I: RESTRUCTURING THE SCHOOL CULTURE

Choosing and developing the *right* staff to work in schools populated by poor minority children is a key to restructuring the school culture. Simply firing one set of teachers and hiring a new set that does not possess the required attributes is counterproductive. These children need neither skeptics nor missionaries; paternalism has no place in a restructured school culture. *Choose* is the critical word; schools populated by these children should not be the "Siberia" to which low-performing teachers are sent as a training ground for the inexperienced and certainly not as a purgatory for teachers who are waiting for a better offer in the suburbs.

Teachers who choose to undergo the work of critical reflection, changing belief systems, and becoming genuinely connected to their students should be amply rewarded. Financial and professional development incentives should be provided for doing the real work involved in school reform. These teachers should be paid well not merely for raising test scores but also for changing students' lives: for inspiring students and helping them to discover their gifts/talents and develop good work habits; they should be rewarded for fostering a love of reading and a commitment to service.

Redefining the Problem

Restructuring the school culture requires defining the problem in a new way by addressing the larger issue of the chronic undereducation of poor minority students. A focus solely on the racial achievement gap is reminiscent of the eugenics movement and studies undertaken in the early 1900s to prove the inferiority of the Negro. Reliance on test scores has replaced measuring the circumference of black skulls (Newby, 1965) as the new evidence of black intellectual inferiority. This total focus on the academic lack of black and brown students is the modern version of reinforcing stereotypical images and perpetuating the ideology of inferiority.

Redefining the problem places the onus for student undereducation on the school. The school staff must ask two critical questions: (1) How have distorted images and erroneous beliefs influenced our current school policies and practices? and (2) How would the experiences of our students be different if they were middle-class students? In answering the second question, focus should remain totally on school-related factors, those factors in the control of the staff, versus problems associated with student poverty, family background, and so on. Redefining the problem assumes that if the educational environment in which these students are schooled changes, educational outcomes for these students will change as well.

Restructuring the school culture and changing institutional as well as individual belief systems will require developing race and class consciousness. It is absolutely necessary to understand the impact of race and class upon the attitudes and behaviors that are found in stigmatizing school environments and to identify the subtle forms of racism and classism that characterize the new color-blind education.

EDUCATION FOR CHANGE

All schools have a lofty vision and mission statement that usually pertains to preparing students for productive citizenship or to effectively participate in the global society. But what should be the purpose of the education of children who are in many ways outsiders in this society? What type of education is best for children who are stigmatized by their racial and social group membership? What type of education will offer them a vision of the practical means they can use to alter their life situations? Finally, what type of knowledge and experience will inspire them to view education not as an individualistic venture designed for material gain but rather as a means of changing both their lives and the communities in which they live?

In a restructured school culture, a philosophy of education must be crafted that is grounded in a belief in the capacity and potential of students as well as one that promotes social justice. At a very pragmatic level, this philosophy of education must address the needs of stigmatized students and the communities from which they come. Like the philosophy of education for freedom espoused by African Americans in the pre-*Brown* era, the purpose of education for the poor minority students attending these schools must be both freedom from poverty and social justice.

An example of a mission statement for a restructured school culture might be: "Our purpose is to produce a highly knowledgeable and skilled individual who views educational attainment as an individual responsibility to the collective good, and who will use his or her knowledge and skills in the role of change agent. Our goal is to educate students who will remain in and change their communities."

PHASE II: REENGAGEMENT OF THE
FAMILY AND COMMUNITY

In the pre-*Brown* era, the schools were the cultural centers of African American communities. As with the church, community life revolved around the school; school plays and programs were community affairs. Academic achievement by students was highlighted and rewarded; parents supported the school by providing much-needed resources. In my experience, parents provided school supplies, made costumes for school plays, carpooled the school band to events, and donated monies when necessary. The connection to the school was central to the community identity.

With desegregation and the loss of community influence and connection, African American parents retreated. Many who were in the first groups to attend desegregated schools hold bitter memories of the school experience and have lost faith in the educational system. Because of their personal experiences, the subsequent negative experiences of their children during the pragmatic phase of desegregation, and the loss of any type of influence and power, African American parents in particular began to distrust the school. With the return of segregated schools to already marginalized communities, the connection between school and community that previously existed was virtually lost.

The schools located in poor minority neighborhoods do not belong to the neighborhoods; they belong to school district, both in a physical and a psychological sense. The restructured school must reestablish a connection with the community in which it is located and reengage the families of students and community in the school. Some charter schools have been very effective in getting minority parents to become involved with the school and to participate actively in the education of their children. Public schools that present a new image of the school and establish a different relationship with parents can accomplish the same.

The building of trust is a key element of the restructured school culture. The trust lost through cumulative negative experiences and the sense of disempowerment related to school must be rebuilt. Because of erroneous beliefs held about parents, new roles must be defined and new rules of engagement employed. Parent involvement must be redefined in terms of a partnership among equals; the belief that all parties have the child's interest in mind and that all have a knowledge base and set of skills that can be effectively used to enhance the educational process.

Accurate images of poor parents and the beliefs held of them must characterize this new relationship with parents. Finally, parents must be convinced that "this school is different," that teachers and administrators genuinely care about their children, and that their children will now have a very different school experience.

The current definition and extent of parent participation, at least for the parents of students attending low-performing schools, is to attend open houses, sign report cards, and show up for disciplinary conferences. A new role, one in which the parent plays a central role—a power-sharing role—must be defined. This role would involve parents in reconstructing the school image and giving input on school policies and practices, especially in the area of discipline, and being able to have a say in the "co-curriculum," discussed further below.

PHASE III: RECONSTRUCTING THE SCHOOL IMAGE

An image of low-performing schools filled with uneducable, out-of-control minority students persists in the public mind, and this image is constantly reinforced by the media. Unfortunately, as microcosms of the larger society, schools for poor minority students embody the same stereotypical view of their students. Rather than being shelters for students who are stigmatized by the larger society, students are trapped by the same images in their schools as in the larger society.

A reconstruction of the school image is a declaration of change in the school's culture and a necessary step in reconstructing the school climate. This, of course, can occur only when new images are held of students and a new belief system is internalized. With trust between the school, parents, and community being restored, the reconstruction of the school's image will necessarily involve a collaboration of all of the parties.

At the institutional level, a "picture of a new reality" must be created and a "reverse form of indoctrination" based upon a counternarrative (Perry et al., 2003) implemented. This new image will be based upon the premise that it is "our truth" and the antithesis of the view held by the media and other outsiders. This reconstructed image will require a shift of focus from "failure" to "potential." Rather than a focus on the grim statistics of who the students "are not," emphasis should be placed on the unique gifts, talents, and transferable skills that make these students the special people that they are. The terms *low-achieving, low-performing,* and *failing* must be removed from the internal vocabulary.

A reconstruction of the image of the student population must be a pervasive undertaking. Through student assemblies, in classrooms, and through dialogues with community members, the idea that "we are not who the media says we are, we are more" must be ingrained in the minds of students and parents. While the reconstructed image realistically must acknowledge the importance of test scores, students must understand that the expectations for them are far greater than test scores would suggest. They must understand that the purpose of their education is to become change agents and that they will be held responsible for making significant contributions to the communities in which they live.

Like the magnet or charter school concept, the reconstructed image should define an academic or service area for which the school will be known. This new image of a progressive rather than a failing school is the one that will be constantly promoted by the school. Perhaps the school will choose to be known for its urban gardening program (related to the science curriculum) or for after-school or weekend shopping for elders (using math skills and service learning). This new image will affirm students' worth and sense of competency while they are also building their academic skills, so that they will have better outcomes in terms of test scores.

PHASE IV: RESTRUCTURING THE SCHOOL CLIMATE

When the institutional belief system is transformed, changes will and must occur in the school climate. A new climate will emerge—one that produces a very different type of learning experience for students. How will the restructured school climate look and feel? In this new climate, students will receive messages that they are valued and respected. High expectations will be held of them and they will be exposed to a rigorous, expansive, and empowering curriculum; they will engage in learning activities that will excite and fully engage them. In this new climate, poor minority students will be given the same learning opportunities as their counterparts in middle-class schools.

THE AFFECTIVE DOMAIN

Fischer and colleagues (1996) state that caste minorities suffer lasting effects of subordinated status; they suggest that subordination leads to low performance in three ways: first through socioeconomic deprivation, second through segregation, and finally through a cultural and psychological process whereby members of subordinate groups understand that they carry a stigma of inferiority based on the wider society's perception of them.

Focus on the affective domain is the cornerstone of a restructured school climate. In such a climate, the development of the whole child and nurturing relationships between teacher and student are considered to be essential for good teaching. The most crucial aspect of the affective focus, however, must be the healing of "stigmatic hurts" suffered by students from caste minority groups. This healing is an essential process that must occur if these students are to develop the academic identity, confidence, and motivation necessary for academic success.

A major goal of activities implemented in the affective domain will be to create a psychologically safe environment for students. In this environment, students will feel respected, trusted, and listened to. They will feel that their culture and selfhood are affirmed. The practice of caring will be demonstrated through personal attention and nurturing relationships. Teachers will, through the quality of their relationships and skills developed in the critical reflection phase of staff development, provide direct intervention to help students overcome "stigmatic hurts." Much can be gained from adopting strategies utilized by teachers in historically black segregated schools.

Teachers who choose to work in schools with poor students from caste minority groups must possess a set of attributes that are essential to developing the quality of relationship needed by students who face daily stigmatization by the larger society. A teacher who is an effective and powerful teacher of these students must possess the following attributes:

- A sense of connectedness: the teacher must feel a sense of "oneness" with the students, families, and community; the teacher must at both an intellectual and feeling level *know* that what affects students' lives will affect his or her life as well. No sense of separation or disconnection from the students or the community can exist.
- A sense of empathy: the teacher must be able to transcend any sense of privilege and be able to "walk in the shoes" of the students he or she teaches.
- Genuineness: an authentic sense of caring is crucial; at the intuitive level, students and parents must *know* if the teacher's smiles, words, and actions are sincere.
- Humility: the ability to acknowledge error; "to give testimony to your redemption"—is necessary.
- Persistence: the ability to accept defeat and to "carry on" in the face of resistance is crucial; it must be remembered that a long history of distrust exists.
- Openness: the ability to face personal demons related to beliefs about race and class and to confront long-held and deep-seated culturally conditioned beliefs.
- "Unconditional positive regard": this, one of the traits renowned psychologist Carl Rogers (1959) advocated as necessary in helping relationships, is crucial. When the image held in mind of the poor and minority groups changes, then unconditional positive regard can be given.
- Respect: the ability to value the knowledge and opinions of both students and their parents; listening to and honoring the knowledge that students and parents can bring is crucial to building a new relationship.
- Courage: the implementation of SRP requires the ability to "go against the grain," "to walk outside the circle," and to some extent to engage in a form of "guerilla" education.
- Commitment to excellence: what will distinguish the effective and powerful teacher of poor children from caste minority groups is simply

wanting to be the best at what he or she does—seeing results, proving the skeptics wrong, and refuting the ideology of inferiority.

THE COGNITIVE DOMAIN

Figuring out what kind of education to provide for poor minority children is not rocket science; it does not require complicated schemes, years of best practices, and reforms that do not work. Mostly, it requires *will* (which is discussed at length in chapter 8); it requires that we have the will to provide the same quality education to poor minority children that is described by Anyon (1987) in her study of *affluent professional* and *executive elite* schools for middle- and upper-class students.

If beliefs that poor minority children are either incapable or undeserving can be overcome, their needs in terms of a quality education can be readily seen. Poor minority children need educational content that is both the *same* and *different* from that provided to middle-class students. Unfortunately, the "value" placed upon the child determines the quality of the curriculum provided. In terms of *sameness*, all children regardless of race or socioeconomic background deserve the following:

- High expectations and no ceiling placed on potential
- High standards of schoolwork—work that is rigorous and challenging
- Schoolwork that allows for individual expressiveness and creativity
- Schoolwork that encourages critical thinking and problem-solving skills
- The opportunity to discover and develop unique gifts and talents
- The development of skills in self-presentation and leadership

EMPOWERMENT EDUCATION

Poor children from caste minority groups also need a *different* co-curriculum—a co-curriculum that deviates from the conventional education prescribed for poor minority students. A co-curriculum combines a basic academic curriculum with an expanded curriculum that meets the specific needs of this student population. A co-curriculum that is a form of *empowerment education* is the hallmark of the school climate restructuring process.

Empowerment is a process of increasing the capacity of individuals or groups to make choices and to transfer these choices into desired actions. For students from caste minority groups, empowerment implies a different philosophy of the purpose of education; education for poor minority children in the twenty-first century must be "education for social justice

---

Textbox 7.2.   Restructuring the School Climate

- Organizational change
- Internal school policies/practices changed
- Co-curriculum ("empowerment education")

---

and change." Empowerment education will include student participation in critical dialogues about the purpose and value of education, counternarratives, and "moral" education.

Character education has become quite popular in schools today, especially those attended by poor minority students. However, a focus on *moral* rather than character education is more pertinent to the needs of poor minority students. Moral education in this context will involve students learning, understanding, and adapting the traits related to such concepts as (1) social justice; (2) cooperation versus competition; and (3) service versus personal gain and materialism.

The goal of empowerment education is not solely individual achievement and upward mobility but rather education as a tool used by the individual to assist in changing and empowering the community from which that individual comes. An empowerment education provides an understanding and the application of learning to social issues and problems. In effect, students participating in empowerment education will understand that personal fulfillment and self-actualization come from becoming change agents and serving their communities. Textbox 7.2 provides an overview of the school climate restructuring process.

COGNITIVE DOMAIN

- An expanded, rigorous curriculum
- Teaching beyond standards
- Discovery/development of gifts/talents
- Application of transferable skills

AFFECTIVE DOMAIN

- Psychologically safe environment
- The practice of caring
- Direct intervention to overcome "stigmatic hurts"

This chapter is not meant to endorse or promote segregated schools. The reality is, however, that we have now returned to legally segregated schools. Outcomes for poor children from caste minority groups cannot and will not change until the quality of their learning environments and school experiences change. The challenge is to discover how to make low-performing post-*Brown* segregated schools attended by poor minority children work. What remains now, after all of the failed schemes and reforms have been tried, is to honestly examine our collective *will* to educate poor minority children in this country.

8

The Fourth Crusade

The Negro needs neither segregated nor mixed schools, what he needs is education.

—W.E.B. DuBois, 1935

The failure to provide first-class education for African American and Latino students has been called one of the central civil rights issues of our time and the main source of ongoing racial inequality in this society (Thernstrom & Thernstrom, 2003). Indeed, rather than being a mechanism for ensuring that the poor and minorities have improved life chances and for preparing leaders who can engage in the process of social change, our schools have become a source for maintaining the status quo and perpetuating the caste system in this nation. Our professed democratic ideals do not equate with our continued failure and lack of will to educate poor minority children in this country.

WHY THE "DISCONNECT"?

In the now almost sixty years since the *Brown* decision, there has been a progression from Jim Crow legally segregated schools, through painful periods of resistance, to pragmatic desegregation, and finally a return to legally segregated schools. The fact that segregation has come full circle in so short a time raises questions that are critical for the collective to answer.

First of all, why does a nation proclaiming that "all men are created equal" accept a return to segregated schools? More importantly, how does a nation that prides itself on being a beacon of democracy tolerate the consistent undereducation of large segments of our population? There is obviously a disconnect between expressed beliefs as opposed to the demonstration of those same democratic ideals. The collective apathy and acceptance of grave inequities toward certain groups in the society is an indication of a *lack of will* to see real change take place in the sociopolitical context of this nation.

A highly skilled workforce and highly educated populace are crucial to the nation's well-being and security, yet there is a collective effort working against the national interests. Why? Why is there no collective will to insist that all children who enter school leave with the best possible education? Below are some possible answers as to why the nation tolerates the return to segregated schools and the undereducation of poor minority children in this country.

- Collectively, there is uncertainty about the *right* of all students to have the same quality of education. Myths of intellectual and cultural inferiority are so ingrained in the national consciousness that there is some uncertainty as to whether the poor and/or minority child really deserves the best education. Despite all the mantras about equality, the belief exists that only the *privileged* are truly worthy of a quality education. No better example of this can be found than the bitter opposition to allowing districts to propose alternative ways of selecting students for gifted programs (e.g., portfolios, expanded views of "giftedness"). Gifted education as well as advanced courses are thought to be solely the domains of the privileged.
- There is collective opposition to open competition. The purpose of caste education remains the same: to keep caste minorities in subservient roles in society and to limit competition in the job market. Providing *all* children with the same quality of education would mean open competition for slots to attend the best universities and get the best jobs. The outcries and opposition to affirmative action (which, in effect, pitted only the brightest of minorities against each other) is indicative of how opposed the collective is to open competition.
- While it cannot be proven that there is a connection, interestingly, as the racial achievement gap began to narrow in the 1970s and 1980s, a reversal of laws related to desegregation began. When the Supreme Court rulings of the 1990s legalized the resegregation of schools, the racial achievement gap began to widen again. The persistence of an education gap prevents open competition in educational opportunities or the job market and ensures the maintenance of the status quo.
- There is a collective comfort with the underclass and their "failure." In a society that promotes the philosophy of individualism, there is little or no sense of connection to others within the society. The poor and caste minorities are "outsiders" and "the other." The collective feels no

connection or responsibility to "them." As was indicated in chapter 3, very harsh views are held of the poor, and of course a history of negative stereotypes is associated with caste minorities in this society. Equally important, in this society, there is a certain aspect of "esteem" bestowed upon those who feel themselves to be better or better off than those at the bottom. That being the case, the privileged have no vested interest in disposing of the means by which they gain a sense of personal worth. Having "failing" schools makes us feel better about our "good" schools, and attending a "good" school reinforces our sense of privilege.

- The sociopolitical context of the nation is based on a model that makes it necessary to have an underclass. On a broad scale, changes in the context within which poor minority children are educated will take a commitment to change the structure of this society. The collective must make a decision that is not only morally right but ultimately in the best interests of the country.

IS THE SITUATION HOPELESS?

Even given the sociopolitical structure of this society, all is not lost; the situation is not hopeless. African American teachers and administrators in the historically black segregated schools effectively educated students and produced leaders in the worst of times. What is needed is a cadre of educators who are brave enough to take the moral high ground and to engage in a process that would transform the structure of education for poor children from caste minority groups—if necessary, one school at a time.

If the nation does not have the will or see the negative consequences of not acting, an enlightened group of educators can begin the process of implementing a program of *socially responsive pedagogy* in their respective school settings. Like African American teachers in Jim Crow days, they may have to circumvent the system; they will have to go against the grain, rebel against the testing that is mostly used to condemn children and their schools, and institute a curriculum and create environments in which poor minority children will be engaged.

Will is resolve; it is the determination to make something occur. In the context of this discussion, *will* is changing the sociopolitical context of schooling for poor children from caste minority groups. Will requires:

- Acknowledging the reality of the caste system in this nation
- Acknowledging the sociopolitical context in which the education of poor minority children takes place in this nation
- Acknowledging the resistance to educating all children in this society and the reasons for this resistance

- Working to change the differential experiences of students from caste minority groups
- Transforming the structure (culture and climate) of schools in which poor children from caste minority groups are educated
- Giving poor students from caste minority groups the full power of educational advantage
- Choosing, for the good of the society, to change the educational structures that maintain the status quo and perpetuate the caste system

A DEMONSTRATION OF WILL

Cuba, our neighbor to the south, is an excellent example of a nation that has the will to provide equal education for all of its children. While the United States and Cuba differ in many ways, including very different political views, Cuba serves as an example of the will to eliminate educational inequities because there are historical similarities between Cuba and the United States. Cuba, like the United States, was a slave society and has a legacy of racism, segregation, discrimination, and social inequities. While still unresolved problems related to racism exist, the Cuban government has made the elimination of inequity in education a top priority. As a result, an egalitarian educational system has emerged.

The Cuban educational system, which is now a source of national pride, had its beginnings after the Cuban Revolution. Before that time, education was the privilege of the middle and upper classes, while the majority of Cuban children remained unschooled. In 1958, over half of all Cuban children were without any schooling at all. Illiteracy was highest in the rural areas, populated mainly by a peasant class.

On January 1, 1961, Cuba's great literacy campaign was launched. The year 1961 was labeled "The Year of Education," and the entire population was mobilized to eradicate illiteracy. Literacy workers of all ages spread throughout the island to teach reading and writing. When the campaign ended on December 31, 1961, a year later, the Cuban illiteracy rate had dropped from 24 to 3 percent. Today, Cuba boasts a 98 percent literacy rate. This achievement has never before occurred anywhere in the world in the history of education; it was the result of a demonstration of will (Aziri, 2000; Huberman & Sweeney, 1969).

Carnoy (2007) compared results of the Latin American Laboratory of Educational Evaluation from Brazil, Chile, and Cuba to determine the reason for the superior performance of Cuba's third and fourth grades in the 1997–1998 thirteen-country UNESCO study of student achievement in language and mathematics. A macroeducational analysis explored the relationship of family, school, and social context factors with differences in student achievement. A second level of analysis focused on school system organization and math education, examining context, teacher education, and supervisors. Finally, the classroom level of Cuban schools was analyzed.

THE SOCIAL CONTEXT OF CUBAN EDUCATION

Two major factors related to *social capital* were identified as contributing to the superior performance of Cuban students:

- *Family human capital*: Parental education (Cuba is a highly literate society across classes) and family social capital—which includes family and community cohesiveness, supportiveness, and networking—facilitate greater student achievement and expectation. I observed the significance of the collectivistic orientation when I explored disciplinary practices in Cuban schools. When a student misbehaves or is not carrying out his or her responsibilities, the student's peer group is first consulted to assist in changing the student's behavior. If peer pressure is not effective, the parents are consulted. Finally, if this fails, the neighbors are asked to influence the parents to change their child's behavior.
- *State-generated social capital*: State policies promote children's welfare, and there is a national focus on education that engenders higher expectations for learning for *all* children in the society.

Together, the Cuban family and state-generated social capital constitute a "social context" or perspective in which *social* inequalities remain a central concern of a government committed to equality and the social policies needed to achieve it. It is Cuba's *sociopolitical* context that most significantly explains why Cuban students score so much higher when compared with students from other regions and which gives them their "academic advantage."

Three crucial elements define and undergird the sociopolitical context in which the education of Cuban children takes place (Lutjens, 2007):

- The Cuban Revolution promised the same education to *all* children regardless of race or class.
- Education is considered to be a basic human *right* in constitutional terms.
- Education is considered to be a *responsibility* of everyone, while the state *guarantees* conditions for equality in education through the centralization of policymaking and welfare functions.

This sociopolitical context includes a centralized system of education, controlled training of teachers, impressive academic skills of teachers, strong instructional supervision of teachers, and high teacher prestige (Carnoy, 2007). For Cuban students, this means:

- Attending schools intensely focused on instruction.
- Being taught by well-trained and regularly supervised teachers.
- A social environment that is dedicated to high academic achievement for *all* social groups.
- A combination of high-quality teaching and high academic expectations that gives Cuban students an education that only upper- and middle-class students receive in other Latin American countries.
- Student achievement at a level higher than socioeconomic background or national income per capita would predict.
- School attendance in a social context that supports children's health and learning.

SCHOOL CLIMATE AND ACADEMIC EXCELLENCE

In the context of this discussion, the analysis of the classroom, the classroom climate, and the practice of "caring" is most significant. Lutjens (2007) describes the results of the aforementioned thirteen-country UNESCO regional study. Quantitative data showed that Cuban students learned twice as much as others in the region; even the lowest 25 percent of Cuban students performed above the regional average. A follow-up study that included school climate (among many variables, such as school management, teaching practices, and so on) examined the qualitative indicators for measuring educational performance.

UNESCO's (Lutjens, 2007) findings indicate that classroom climate was judged to be the most significant factor in explaining the differential performance of Cuban students. A positive school climate in Cuban schools is associated with schools having outstanding results and provides a view of the culture of schooling in Cuba. Ninety-seven percent of Cuban students reported a positive classroom environment, in contrast to 51 percent of the students in other countries. In these high-achieving Cuban schools:

- Kindness is a recurrent theme and is characteristic of the climate.
- Students feel good about being in school, are treated with kindness, and like to go to class.
- Teachers are close to but demanding of students; they use colloquial and affective language, call students by their first names, and demonstrate confidence in the ability of all to learn.
- Teachers stimulate and reinforce the active participation of students.
- Teachers recognize individual differences in students.

The "practice of care" is a central component of the sociopolitical context in which Cuban students are educated. Lutjens (2007) describes nine characteristics of "caring "classrooms in Cuban schools:

- Respect and care in school through a curriculum that stresses social justice
- Strong moral discipline
- Teaching values through curriculum
- Ethical reflection
- Academic responsibility and good work habits (the conscience of craft)
- Cooperative learning
- A democratic classroom environment
- Conflict resolution

In Cuban schools, where a *pedagogy of tenderness* or *caring* is advocated, the affective domain is considered to be as important as the cognitive domain in terms of academic success (Lutjens, 2007). The importance of and demonstration of the "practice of care " that is described as being characteristic of Cuban schools is very similar to that which existed in good historically black segregated schools.

The Cuban demonstration of the will to create learning environments in which social inequities are eliminated offers lessons that, if embraced, can serve as a model for transforming the educational context of poor minority students in this country. The following lessons are worth noting:

- Schooling must be a national priority.
- Education and equity in schooling are the means for eliminating inequality in society.
- Equality of education must be regarded as a right for all groups in the society.
- The national government must guarantee equality of education.
- High expectations must be demonstrated for all students.
- The affective domain and the "practice of caring" are critical aspects of the school climate for students from collectivistic cultures (e.g., caste minorities).
- Equitable education for all is a means of maximizing a country's human potential and investing in the nation's own interests.

REAL EDUCATIONAL REFORM

This book presents the reality of the context in which the masses of poor children from caste minority groups are schooled in our nation today. They attend schools that are stigmatized by the larger society, and they face the same stigmatization within the school setting itself. They attend schools that limit rather than expand their intellectual potential, and they are subjected to a continuous barrage of tests that only serve to reinforce an image of their inferiority. In addition, many must work daily within a classroom climate that can only be described as hostile.

The desegregation process as implemented was obviously not the answer to providing an equal and quality education for minority students. Morris (1999) suggests that desegregation policies should be reconceptualized and should focus on equity in education for low-income students who still attend and will continue to attend predominately minority schools. Morris contends that the quality of the education received by low-income African American students who attend predominately African American schools is the true barometer for gauging whether the vision of *Brown* has been realized.

Instituting national standards and pouring millions of dollars into creating the same programs and strategies based upon deficit theory and rooted in the ideology of inferiority will not improve educational outcomes for the students sentenced to languish in our newly segregated schools. Real school reform requires the will to make substantial and structural changes in the way that we educate students from caste minorities.

Ogbu (1978) suggests that the goal of school reform should be to eliminate both the obvious and subtle ways in which schools prevent members of caste minorities from receiving the quality of education that would enable them to compete and play a constructive role in society. School reform, therefore, should be part of the overall effort to dismantle the caste system, and schools should be agents of the equalization of social status.

THE FOURTH CRUSADE

We have come a long distance since the beginnings of the first crusade by ex-slaves to seek freedom and education for freedom. But unfortunately, some sixty years after *Brown*, there is the recognition that the struggle for educational equity is far from over, especially for poor minority children who are consigned to post-*Brown* segregated schools. A fourth crusade is now necessary to ensure that black and brown children in this nation are guaranteed a quality education in the schools that they attend, albeit segregated schools.

The fourth crusade that is needed asks schools to assume the role of agents of equalization of social status. This crusade requires a cadre of dedicated, excellently trained professionals who will descend upon the new segregated schools with the purpose of doing what the larger society seems unwilling to do: eliminating social and economic inequities in this society. The fourth crusade will require that youth from broken, neglected, and forgotten neighborhoods be educated to become agents of change in their own communities. Education in these schools will be regarded as a collective responsibility; the purpose of education being the liberation from poverty and social injustice.

This crusade will need educators who are neither derisive nor paternalistic but who feel and believe in their connectedness to their students and the communities in which they teach. They will have done the work of critical reflection and will not be afraid to examine and challenge the flaws inherent in *color-blind* education. The will understand the significance and value of *socially responsive pedagogy.*

The fourth crusade is not unlike the previous crusades carried out by African Americans for free public education, the maintenance of schools for African Americans in the face of segregation and discrimination, and the desegregation of schools. It will also require the action of citizens who believe that equal educational opportunity is the right of all children. Civil rights leader Bob Moses has called for an organized movement to demand that the Constitution be amended to make quality education a constitutionally guaranteed right (Perry, 2010). It is imperative that black and brown communities join in this effort to finally secure equal educational opportunities for their children.

EDUCATIONAL EQUITY AND THE NATIONAL INTEREST

Education is considered to be the main vehicle for social mobility in modern democracies; it is the means by which people earn more and gain higher social status. Among eight democracies studied, the United States was found to have the lowest mobility rate (Wilkinson & Pickett, 2009). Inequality in schooling and especially the undereducation of large segments of the population (poor students from caste minority groups) are contributing factors to the lack of mobility in this society. Post-*Brown* segregated schools in which stigmatizing environments are the norm actually perpetuate rather than facilitate movement out of the underclass.

Cortes (2010) suggests that the demands of the twenty-first-century economy and the growing population of Social Security recipients makes it in our national interest to invest in education and to educate *all* of our children well. Studies have documented that a well-educated workforce earns higher wages, pays higher taxes, requires few governmental services, and generates economic growth through production and consumption.

While at the moment there seems to be very little concern about the failure of schools to educate poor minority children, a very high price will be paid by all of us as a nation in the future. Segregated schools are inherently unequal schools, and unequal schools contribute to and maintain inequality in our society. Continuing to maintain schools that perpetuate the underclass threatens the well-being of our society. Studies have shown that health and social problems are more common in unequal societies (Wilkinson & Pickett, 2009).

No change, of course, can occur if there is no *will* to do so. The will to transform schools requires a nation that does not need an underclass; the esteem of the middle class should not be dependent upon "at least not being one of *them.*" Instead, it requires a nation that embraces open competition in education and employment and that is dedicated to overcoming its commitment to hypocrisy, denial, and illusions. There is always a price to be paid for failing to take the moral high ground. Will the price be the loss of status in the world because of a lack of ability to compete? Will the nation stay mired in ideologies designed to justify immoral deeds while other nations march ahead? What will be the fate of the nation? Is there the will to change?

Finally, a large segment of the students who attended my pre-*Brown* segregated school lived in public housing, known as "the projects." Out of the projects, in my class alone, came a brilliant mathematician, teachers, social workers, government personnel, and successful business owners. When I consider the state of poor black and brown students who attend post-*Brown* segregated schools, I question what would have become of my classmates had they been students in today's segregated schools. Would their abilities and talents have gone unnoticed? Would their potential have been shrouded by flawed images of them and their families, erroneous beliefs about their abilities, or low expectations for what they could achieve?

It is painful to look into the faces of children who are languishing in stigmatizing environments and yet know what could be possible for them. Through no fault of their own, these children will never have a chance to claim even a small piece of the American dream; their lives are already being configured within the school walls. Their undereducation will take them no farther than a job at the local fast-food shop or, worse yet, into the school-to-prison pipeline. Morris (1999) is correct when he says that the "real retreat" from *Brown* will occur if we ignore the students who now attend our resegregated schools.

Appendix

Miss Thompson's Wisdom

Wisdom is the ability to discern inner qualities and relationships. It is this ability to really "see" a child that makes a great teacher. With a teacher's wisdom, the gifts, talents, and potential within even the poorest and most belligerent student can be discovered and developed through the practice of caring. A teacher with this wisdom can create a learning environment in which each child's worth is affirmed and children develop a sense of competency and confidence in their abilities.

A teacher with this type of wisdom can change a child's life for the better forever. One such teacher was Mrs. Evelyn Lawrence, or Miss Thompson, as she was called, my second grade teacher at the Carnegie School in Marion, Virginia. Miss Thompson was such an exceptional teacher that it is difficult to find words to express her power and influence upon the hundreds of students she taught.

In chapter 6, the culture and climate of "good" historically black segregated schools was described. Carnegie was one of those good schools; the single most important aspect of the school were the hard-working, dedicated teachers who set out to prove to black students that despite all the myths and stereotypes, they were special, had much to offer, and were expected to make contributions to society commensurate with their talents and abilities. Miss Thompson embodied all of the qualities of the teachers who made good historically black segregated schools places of refuge and inspiration.

ABOUT MISS THOMPSON

Mrs. Evelyn Thompson Lawrence was a teacher for forty-four years before retiring. She taught for twenty-six years at the all-black Carnegie High School and eighteen years at Marion Primary School after schools were desegregated. She received a bachelor of science degree in Music and English from West Virginia State University and a master's degree in Music from the University of Michigan. Evelyn Lawrence was the first teacher, black or white, with a master's degree to teach in a classroom in the Smyth County school system.

African American teachers lost their jobs all across the South when the desegregation of schools occurred. Evelyn Thompson Lawrence, however, was the first African American teacher to be hired to teach in a desegregated school. She taught at Marion Primary School until she retired. In 1970, she was one of three educators selected from the Ninth District to work on the Virginia State Department of Education's Standards of Learning Skills (SOS) project.

Retirement has not meant that Miss Thompson would be any the less busy. Just as she did at Carnegie and then at Marion Primary School, each year she writes and produces an operetta for children with dialogue, music, and elaborate costumes and stage settings. She authored the "Directory of African American Students and Teachers in all Smyth County Schools, 1906–1965" in 1994, and in 2006, she established the Mount Pleasant Heritage Museum to honor the outstanding past and present contributions of African Americans in Smyth County.

Miss Thompson has received many awards and honors. She was the 1985 recipient of the Marion Rotary Club Citizen of the Year Award; she was honored with "Evelyn Lawrence Days" by the Marion Town Council in 2007; in 2008 and 2009 she was honored as one of Virginia Mountains' Most Beautiful People for making a positive difference in the lives of others. Perhaps her greatest honor was being acknowledged for her lifetime achievements by the Commonwealth of Virginia General Assembly House of Delegates in 2008. On September 12, 2010, the Community Heritage Celebration Committee presented a tribute to Evelyn Lawrence, honoring her as a local legend.

I feel honored that Evelyn Lawrence, whom we called Miss Thompson, has chosen to share the wisdom gained from her many years of working with children, youth, and adults in the school, church, and community. Poor minority children are failing to become adequately educated in our schools today. There is much that can be learned from Miss Thompson about how to reach and teach these students.

What follows are Miss Thompson's answers to questions I posed about how she and other teachers at the all-black Carnegie School were able to produce students who were academic achievers and went on to become leaders in their respective fields. As suggested in chapter 6, there is much that can be learned from these teachers about how to teach poor minority students in resegregated schools. Miss Thompson has provided the wisdom required to create the environments in which poor minority students will thrive, achieve, and reach their full potential.

MRB: To begin, help me get a feel for what it was like to teach at the all-black Carnegie School.

Miss Thompson: First of all, when I look at the sad state of public education today for African American children and youth, I yearn for a return to those wonderful, halcyon days, eons ago; days that can never be again but days when I was fortunate enough to be a teacher in the Carnegie High School in Marion, Virginia.

Carnegie High School, the only high school in Smyth County for African Americans, was the most unique school in the county and existed for thirty-four years, from 1931 to 1965. Four teachers (only four, for twenty years) were responsible for teaching all subjects, grades 1 through 11; the total high school enrollment was approximately 120 students.

This circumstance was a big challenge for these few teachers. All other schools in the county were provided with one teacher per grade; not so at Carnegie. There were three grades per classroom for the primary and intermediate teachers, and the other five high school grades were taught by the remaining two teachers. These three were hard-working, caring, dedicated educators. The four of us sought to challenge and to educate our student body through a positive enriched curriculum.

Mr. Dabney (the principal and high school science teacher) did not have access to the costly, needed lab equipment that other county schools had. There was a lot of innovation, serendipity; creating simple, inexpensive experiments. Teachers used their personal money for equipment and students found useful supplies in their homes.

Each year upon graduation, the Carnegie High grad was expected to measure up academically with the graduates of all other Smyth County schools. And surprisingly, they did! How how how?

All teachers throughout the entire period were well-educated, patient, hard-working women and men who daily performed admirably in their respective classrooms under difficult circumstances. [Note: Even though all Carnegie teachers had bachelor's degrees from outstanding institutions, their salaries were less than those of other county teachers (white), who had only normal degrees (two years) and others even less.] I earned a master of music degree from the University of Michigan but was paid the salary of bachelor of arts teachers, even though I protested.

MRB: Describe your relationship with the parents of your students.

Miss Thompson: We had good relationships with the parents of the students that we taught. The parents were supportive of my academic programs, art, music, and drama. I regularly informed them personally and by report card of their children's progress, positive or negative. Homework was a daily "must" even in the primary grades, and parents were most helpful and cooperative.

In my early years at Carnegie, the school board did not provide any funding for resources or equipment. Many of my parents were so very supportive; I did not hesitate to let them know of our classroom needs. They were kind enough to collect (usually thrown-away) items for activities, such as popsicle sticks, cardboard milk-bottle tops, chicken and turkey feathers, colored beads, decorative paper plates and cups, wallpaper sample books, shoeboxes, pretty small samples of cloth (yard goods), dried pasta in all shapes. Some parents even donated scissors.

With encouragement, it was amazing how pupils created magical pictures, murals, and dioramas from the assortment of "stuff" listed above. The artistic results gave a boost to the children's pride and self-worth.

MRB: Describe the relationship that you had with your students.

Miss Thompson: With my students, I used a consistent code of discipline, making it clear that as a teacher my goal was to guide and to inspire them to always do their academic best. I realized that I needed to be aware of and to address the children's individual differences. At informal times, it was fun to interact with my pupils in humorous or informal ways. Discipline was not a serious problem, for children were taught at home to respect and obey teachers, who in most instances were positive role models for the students.

In her first comments, Miss Thompson touched upon a major similarity between pre-and post-*Brown* schools; the same expectations and standards were and are held for the students who attended segregated schools despite the lack of equal resources and advantages. As in pre-*Brown* days, poor minority students who attend post-*Brown* segregated schools are evaluated according to the same criteria with no regard to inequitable conditions, including chronic undereducation.

Miss Thompson: Let me take you to my Carnegie classroom from the 1940s to the mid-1960s. Mandatory school desegregation came to the state of Virginia in 1965, and Carnegie High School closed its doors forever that June.

The former school was converted into the Mountain Community Action Program Head Start after the school closed; as with many other all-black historically segregated schools, nothing remains of the rich culture that the school provided. Miss Thompson however, established a Carnegie High School Alumni Reunion that meets biannually.

Miss Thompson: When I walked into my very first classroom, there were forty-seven young girls and boys in grades 1 through 3, approximately fifteen students per grade. My goal was to help these children achieve their academic best. And there was more: every afternoon I taught high school music. Each spring, I taught music to grades 1 through 7, and they performed in the annual county music festival and earned high grades. (In neighboring counties, blacks were not allowed to participate in white festivals.) This would require approximately 180 hours yearly of my time taken away from my primary pupils. I would devise lesson plans for that period, and the principal would supply two especially selected high school girls to "hold forth" in my classroom.

One might ask how there could be any academic measure of success? Had there not been teamwork, dedication, and perseverance, such could not have been accomplished.

The common goal of high academic achievement and collective responsibility for that achievement was evident in Miss Thompson's remarks and experience at Carnegie.

Miss Thompson: How did I begin? First of all, I knew that like fingerprints or DNA, no two pupils were identical, perhaps very much alike but not identical. (I always kept a notebook listing the personal characteristics of each student.) There was the brassy, the shy, the bully, the lovable, the insecure child. A different approach for each would be necessary: one of many other remedies or approaches was to use various characters in appropriate stories to help children recognize and improve their shortcomings. Also, one-on-one talk with each student was always helpful.

MRB: Miss Thompson, what do you believe is the teacher's role?

Miss Thompson: As a teacher, I feel that the purpose of education is to instill within the student a sense or feeling of confidence and self-worth and a desire to be a future worthwhile citizen through consistency, patience, and perseverance as the goal.

We immediately see how significant focus on the affective domain was in Miss Thompson's approach to teaching. In fact, she began with the affective domain, which enabled her to have success in the cognitive domain. In her comments below, we hear the importance of using strategies to directly intervene in helping students from a caste minority group to overcome "stigmatic hurts." She used a variety of strategies, including "counternarratives" to offset the stigmatizing stereotypes to which the students were subjected and to provide inspiration for success. But in "critical conversations," she also told them about the reality of life as a black person in this country.

MRB: What strategies did you use to help your students overcome the stigma imposed by racial stereotypes?

Miss Thompson: First of all, I tried to make it clear to my children that they were important and that they owed it to themselves to prove their inherent abilities. Even though the playing field was uneven, unfair because of race, my motto was "Never give up, just try harder." African American children before the 1960s learned very early what it meant to be black. Even in the Primary grades, 1, 2, and 3, I felt compelled to make my little ones aware of the fact that the type of life awaiting them in the future depended on their beliefs, attitudes, skills, and values. I used various approaches for help:

- To combat the perception of feeling inferior because of race, I cited family or community adults who, despite hardships, have endured and have made notable contributions.
- Black history was a mechanism: I would use George W. Carver, Booker T. Washington, and Harriet Tubman as examples of those who were able to triumph over adversities.
- The African American media (newspapers and magazines) was used to reinforce racial pride.
- I used white newspapers showing photos of winning black sports players to prove that the only way for the athletes to earn such acclaim was for them to be two or three times better at the game than their white teammates, and so on.

MRB: What beliefs and attitudes did you feel were essential for your students? What strategies did you use to help them develop these attitudes?

Miss Thompson: African American students need to develop certain attitudes in order to be successful. I taught them that achieving success requires that one must be patient, persevere, and expect to suffer hardship and inequity to reach the desired goal. Pupils need to realize that we African Americans live in a country where we are considered a minority, and that is not controlled by us. Therefore, to compete for a job or career opportunities, the black citizen has to be two or three times more competent than other citizens, which means that black children need to work harder to measure up.

I also used stories for encouragement like "Hans Brinker and the Silver Skates." Hans won the ice-skating race and was given the prized silver skates because he practiced every day for the race with a brick strapped on each leg, skating with "all his might." On the day of the contest, he removed the bricks and skated with "all his might," thus winning. This is a good sensible strategy for success for minority students.

Finally, I used myself as an example. When I enrolled in a predominately all-white university, I knew that I would have to earn high grades to be able to remain. I always arrived at the classroom early. I always sat on the front row, or up front. I always made it a point to speak in class every class, every day, or ask a question so that I would be remembered by the professor. When the class was asked to read and report on five books, I would read and report on six or seven books. It all paid off. Very often I would be numbered with the ones exempted from certain exams.

MRB: How did you keep students engaged in the learning process?

Miss Thompson: My challenge; I always felt the necessity to pique the interest and curiosity of each child in my classroom. A child with no incentive is in a position of "stalemate"; he or she doesn't care about anything pro or con. With a schedule full enough for three teachers, I attempted daily to do justice for each group, for academics were so important. The key was to never allow the pupil to lose interest.

I always presented to my students exciting projects and programs that related to fun and fancy but also tied in or related to academics. For instance, in Physical Education, when we learned new folk rhythms (England, Ireland, and France), we also did research about the country, its geographical location, customs, costumes, and the like. I did much map study.

The students loved to create units—such as Indian villages, farms, holidays, cities, towns—using the sand table and bulletin board for displays. With all sorts of beads, wooden blocks, colored paper, cardboard cartons, round milk tops, Popsicle sticks, scissors, crayons, glue, and tempera, pupils constructed collages, pictures, and 3D items for their units.

At the close of each year, I produced on stage a big operetta with dialogue, music, dances, costumes, and stage décor. Parents were most helpful. Pupils looked forward to the excitement, the glamour of the upcoming productions.

In a multigrade classroom, some subjects could be combined to teach all three groups collectively, such as Social Studies, Science, Health, and Physical Education. But spelling and the 3R's are courses that must be taught to individual grades. That meant that while I was in session with one grade group, the two other groups were without me. What did I do?

It was necessary to provide wholesome learning experiences for these two groups. My answer was *centers*; in the rear of my very large classroom, I set up interest centers: nooks, a sand table, and tables with a variety of materials for quiet individual or group (usually two students) study. There were centers for many interests: reading, science, jigsaw and other puzzles, creative writing, games (dominoes, Chinese checkers), art (drawing, coloring, painting), worksheets (math and language arts) and potted plants (flowers and ferns).

Each center area was designed to promote learning experiences. From my home library, I brought my pictorial *World Book Encyclopedia* set and placed the volumes on the very bottom shelf nearest the floor. Children loved to explore the fascinating pictures while sitting on little rug samples I placed on the floor. It's surprising that a few third-graders could read parts of the book commentary. Others asked questions.

How much more exciting and engaging this pre-*Brown* overcrowded classroom with few resources sounds compared with the dull learning environments forced upon poor minority students as they daily must endure a test-preparation curriculum. It is ironic that even during the era of Jim Crow, in Miss Thompson's classroom, students were not subjected to the class-based or caste education that is forced upon poor minority students in post-*Brown* segregated schools.

MRB: What do you believe are the most desirable traits in a teacher?

Miss Thompson:
- Love: For a teacher, love is the key. All children, even the child who may appear to lack the same ability as others, can sense the degree of a teacher's affection or the lack of it. I thoroughly enjoyed being a classroom teacher because I loved working with children. Before integration, in the 1940s, Dr. A. G. Macklin, a Negro member of the Virginia State Department of Education, heard my Carnegie High School chorus perform. He

was so impressed that he offered me the position of Virginia State Supervisor of Music, for African American schools of course. Many other qualified teachers would have "jumped at the chance" because of the notoriety, the honor, and the salary increase. I declined the lucrative opportunity, for I didn't want to lose my association with children.

- Maintaining pupil curiosity is the key. The teacher should generate and maintain the interest of the children. There must be constant projects to inspire children to think, collect, research, and create. Centers were, for me, invaluable.
- Finding remedies: What about the child who realizes he cannot cope, cannot keep up with his class? He either withdraws and is sullen and silent or becomes a bully. What can a teacher do? My experiences helped me learn that even in the most incorrigible child, there is the semblance of "one" virtue.
  — For the bully: Give him a "peacekeeping" task but monitor him closely. Such a job makes him feel "special," and he will protect, not harm, the smaller child.
  — For struggling readers: In the case of a boy I'll call Jay, I learned that he was a master at clay sculpture. He never learned to read, but he was able to succeed at something that no student or teacher could. Jay did a whole dinosaur clay unit for the Annual County Festival. I openly praised him often. He felt important.
  — "Jack" never learned to read either. But his beautiful, sweet, ethereal singing voice brought tears to my heart. If he had been in Europe, he could have easily been chosen as a Vienna Choir Boy. I had him do solos often. Children like the three above need acceptance, praise, and the feeling of belonging.
  — For the shy child: I was able to bring out my shy child by having her speak through her puppet until she felt comfortable using "her own voice."
  — Carnegie teachers did bus duty a whole week at a time. I found that bus duty afforded me the opportunity to informally talk and listen to a wide variety of students. I learned much about their problems as well as their aspirations.

Miss Thompson thus described what the practice of "caring" is all about; providing love, acceptance, praise, and a sense of belonging. As stated earlier, this sense of caring is especially crucial for children who are stigmatized by the larger society. What was done routinely and accepted as simply a part of teaching in pre-*Brown* segregated schools must be cultivated in the environments of post-*Brown* segregated schools. Miss Thompson could not end her interview without discussing "chapel."

Miss Thompson: One of the most rewarding pupil experiences at Carnegie High School was "chapel," initiated in 1931, when the school first opened. What was chapel? Every Friday morning at 11:00 A.M., the period before lunch,

I would play a lively march tune on the auditorium piano. All grades, one through eleven, marched regiment style, high stepping, lower grades in front, and high school in the rear. I can still hear the rhythmic, steady beat of happy feet keeping perfect time with the music.

Each week a different grade group presented the program on the stage. I considered most of them to be "true gems." How great it would have been if, back in those days, we had the technology of taping these events.

Chapel was a unifying experience. There was a mutual respect that bonded the whole school group into one loving academic family. When each class performed on stage, the others listened, were attentive, and learned. Just think of the advantages in later life afforded our Carnegie student body. Most of them have been able to perform efficiently without fear of failure. They, today, are great teachers and leaders in many fields.

Chapel was that aspect of the historically black segregated school experience that developed in students the sense of competency and confidence needed to take academic and social risks, to compete, and to learn the skills needed to lead. Of all the aspects of the "culture" of pre-*Brown* segregated schools that were lost during desegregation, the loss of chapel remains the greatest deprivation to students who otherwise have no opportunity to learn the crucial social and leadership skills that are necessary cultural capital in the larger society.

MRB: What advice can you give to teachers who teach poor minority students?

Miss Thompson: To the teacher of poor minority children, I say a child's best hours of the day are spent at school, not at home. So:

- The teacher should listen to him or her. He or she may need an assuring pat or hug.
- In your center, select teams where the strong student helps the weak student in reading, math, and spelling.
- The problem student will begin his antics at the outset. Be firm and unchanging with him. Make it clear to him that he will conform to school rules just like any other student. Then consult the parents, school nurse, principal, and counselor. See what triggers his behavior.
- Spanking is no longer permitted in the classroom, so other means must be sought to address the problem such as (1) continual talking to the troublemaker, (2) reducing his privileges, or (3) reseating him to an area where you ask him to think about his unacceptable behavior, and decide if he can pledge to himself to do better.

MRB: Miss Thompson, any final comments?

Miss Thompson: The most important thing for educators to remember is that "a child is like a piece of paper on which each of us writes a little."

References

Alexander, K., Entwisle, D., & Thompson, M. (1987). School performance, status relations, and the structure of sentiment: Bringing the teacher back in. *American Sociological Review, 52,* 665–82.

Anderson, J. (1988). *The education of blacks in the South, 1860–1935.* Chapel Hill: University of North Carolina Press.

Anderson, J., & Byrne, D. (2004). *The unfinished agenda of* Brown v. Board of Education. Hoboken, NJ: John Wiley & Sons.

Anyon, J. (1980). Social class and the hidden curriculum of work. *Journal of Education, 1,* 67–92.

Arganbright, J. (1983). Teacher expectations: A critical factor for student achievement. *NASSP Bulletin, 67*(464), 93–95.

Aziri, M. (2000). *Cuba today and tomorrow: Reinventing socialism.* Gainesville: University Press of Florida.

Baker, R. S. (2006). *Paradoxes of desegregation: African American struggles for educational equity in Charleston, South Carolina, 1926–1972.* Columbia: University of South Carolina Press.

Bamburg, J. (1994). *Raising expectations to improve student learning.* Oak Brook, IL: North Central Regional Educational Laboratory.

Bartley, N. (1997). *The rise of massive resistance: Race and politics in the South during the 1950's.* Baton Rouge: Louisiana State University Press.

Bireda, M. (2010). *Cultures in conflict: Eliminating racial profiling.* Lanham, MD: Rowman & Littlefield.

Boger, J. and Orfield, G. (Eds). *School Resegregation: Must the South turn back?* Chapel Hill, NC: The University of North Carolina Press.

Bonilla-Silva, E. (2010). *Racism without racists: Color-blind racism & racial inequality in contemporary America* (3rd ed.). Lanham, MD: Rowman & Littlefield.

Boykin, A.W., & Jones, J. (2004). The psychological evolution of black children's education since *Brown*. In J. Anderson & D. Byrne (Eds.). *The unfinished agenda of* Brown v. Board of Education. New York: John Wiley & Sons.

Bullock, H. A. (1967). *A history of Negro education in the South: From 1619 to the present.* New York: Praeger.

Carnoy, M. (2007). *Cuba's academic advantage: Why students in Cuba do better in school.* Stanford, CA: Stanford University Press.

Cecelski, D. (1994). *Along Freedom Road: Hyde County North Carolina and the fate of black schools in the South.* Chapel Hill: University of North Carolina Press.

Clotfelter, C. (2004). *After* Brown: *The rise and retreat of school desegregation.* Princeton, NJ: Princeton University Press.

Cortes, E., Jr. (2010). Quality education as a civil right: Reflections. In T. Perry, R. P. Moses, J. T. Wynne, E. Cortes Jr., & L. Delpit (Eds.). *Quality education as a constitutional right: Creating a grassroots movement to transform public schools.* Boston: Beacon Press.

Del Pilar O'Cadiz, M., Lindquist Wong, P., & Torres, C. (1998). *Education and democracy: Paulo Freire, social movements, and educational reform in Sao Paulo.* Boulder, CO: Westview Press.

Dempsey, V., & Noblit, G. (1993). The demise of caring in an African American community: One consequence of school desegregation. *Urban Review, 25,* 47–61.

Diamond, J., Randolph, A., & Spillane, J. (2004). Teachers' expectations and sense of responsibility for student learning: The importance of race, class, and organizational habitus. *Anthropology & Education Quarterly, 35*(1), 75–98.

DuBois, W.E.B. (1935). Does the Negro need separate schools? *Journal of Negro Education, 4,* 328–32.

Epstein, J. (1985). After the bus arrives: Resegregtion in desegregated schools. *Journal of Social Issues, 41*(3), 23–43.

Erikson, E. (1968). *Childhood and society.* New York: W. W. Norton.

Eyler, J., Cook, V., & Ward, L. (1983). Re-segregation within desegregated schools. In C. Rossell & W. Hawley (Eds.). *The consequences of school desegregation.* Philadelphia: Temple University Press.

Fairclough, A. (2007). *A class of their own: Black teachers in the segregated South.* Cambridge, MA: Harvard University Press.

Ferguson, A. A. (2001). *Bad boys: Public schools in the making of black masculinity.* Ann Arbor: University of Michigan Press.

Ferguson, R. (1998). Teachers' perceptions and expectations and the Black-White test score gap. In C. Jencks & M. Phillips (Eds.). *The Black-White test score gap.* Washington, DC: Brookings Institution Press.

Ferguson, R. F. (2002). *Addressing racial disparities in high-achieving suburban schools.* North Central Regional Educational Laboratory. From www.ncrel.org/policy/pubs/html/pivol13/dec2002b.htm/.

Fischer, C. S., Hout, M., Jankowski, M. S., Lucas, S. R., Swidler, A., & Voss, K. (1996). *Inequality by design: Cracking the bell curve myth.* Princeton: Princeton University Press.

Foster, M. (1990). The politics of race: Through the eyes of African-American teachers. *Journal of Education, 172*(3), 123–41.

Foster, M. (1997). *Black teachers on teaching.* New York: New Press.

Gans, H.(1995). *The war against the poor.* New York, NY: Basic Books.

Gibson, M. A., & Ogbu, J. U. (Eds). (1991). *Minority status and schooling: A comparative study of immigrant and involuntary minorities.* New York: Garland.

Holliday, B. (1985). Differential effects of children's self-perceptions and teachers' perceptions on black children's academic achievement. *Journal of Negro Education, 54*(1), 71–81.

Huberman, L., & Sweeny, P. M. (1969). *Socialism in Cuba.* New York: Modern Reader Paperbacks.

Hyman, I., & Snook, P. A. (1999). *Dangerous schools: What we can do about the physical and emotional abuse of our children.* San Francisco: Jossey-Bass, Inc. Publishers.

Irvine, R. W., & Irvine, J. J. (1983). The impact of the desegregation process on the education of black students: Key variables. *Journal of Negro Education, 52*(4), 410–22.

Jackson, J. T. (1999). What are the real risk factors for African American children? *Phi Delta Kappan, 81*(4), 308–12.

Jones, F. (1981). *A traditional model of educational excellence.* Washington, DC: Howard University Press.

Jussim, L., & Harber, K. (2005). Teacher expectations and self-fulfilling prophecies: Knowns and unknowns, resolved and unresolved controversies. *Personality and Social Psychology Review, 9*(2), 131–55.

Kozol, J. (2005). *The shame of the nation: The restoration of apartheid schooling in America.* New York: Three Rivers Press.

Lee, Y. (1991). Koreans in Japan and the United States. In M. A. Gibson & J. U. Ogbu (Eds.). *Minority status and schooling: A comparative study of immigrant and involuntary minorities.* New York: Garland.

Lomack, G. (2004). Organizational behavior and the consequences for the culturally different. In S. Goodman & K. Carey (Eds.). *Critical multicultural conversations.* Cresskill, NJ: Hampton Press.

Lustig, M., & Koester, J. (1996). *Intercultural competence: Interpersonal communication across cultures* (2nd ed.). New York: HarperCollins College Publishers.

Lutjens, S. (2007). (Re)reading Cuban educational policy: Schooling and the Third Revolution. In I. Epstein (Ed.). *Recapturing the personal: Essays on education and embodied knowledge in comparative perspective.* Charlotte, NC: Information Age Publishing.

Meier, K., Stewart, J. Jr., & England, R. (1989). *Race, class, and education: The politics of second-generation discrimination.* Madison: University of Wisconsin Press.

Morris, J. E. (1999). What is the future of predominately black urban schools? The politics of race in urban education policy. *Phi Delta Kappan, 81*(4), 316–19.

Morris, V. G., & Morris, C. L. (2002). *The price they paid: Desegregation in an African American community.* New York: Teachers College Press.

Muse, B. (1964). *Ten years of prelude: The story of integration since the Supreme Court's 1954 decision.* New York: Viking Press.

Network of Regional Desegregation Centers (1989). *Resegregation of public schools: The third generation.* Washington, DC: U.S. Department of Education.

Newby, I. A.(1965). *Jim Crow's defense: Anti-Negro thought in America 1900–1930.* Baton Rouge: Louisiana State University.

O'Cadiz, P., Wong, P., & Torres, C. (1998). *Education and democracy: Paulo Freire, social movements, and educational reform in Sao Paulo.* Boulder, CO: Westview Press.

Ogbu, J. U. (1978). *Minority education and caste: The American system in cross-cultural perspective.* New York: Academic Press.

Orfield, G. (2005). The southern dilemma: Losing *Brown,* fearing *Plessey.* In J. Boger & G. Orfield (Eds.). *Must the South turn back?* Chapel Hill: University of North Carolina Press.

Orfield, G., & Eaton, S. (1996). *Dismantling desegregation: The quiet reversal of* Brown v. Board of Education. New York: New Press.

Packard, J. (2002). *American nightmare: The history of Jim Crow.* New York: St. Martin's Press.

Patterson, J. (2001). Brown v. Board of Education: *A civil rights milestone and its troubled legacy.* New York: Oxford University Press.

Perry, T. (2010). The historical and contemporary foundations for Robert Moses's call to make quality education a constitutionally guaranteed right. In T. Perry, R. P. Moses, J. T. Wynne, E. Cortes Jr., & L. Delpit (Eds.). *Quality education as a constitutional right: Creating a grassroots movement to transform public schools.* Boston: Beacon Press.

Perry, T., Moses, R. P., Wynne, J. T., Cortes, E. Jr., & Delpit, L. (Eds.). (2010). *Quality education as a constitutional right: Creating a grassroots movement to transform public schools.* Boston: Beacon Press.

Perry, T., Steele, C., & Hilliard, A. III. (2003). *Young, gifted, and black: Promoting high achievement among African-American students.* Boston: Beacon Press.

Peters, W. (1987). *A class divided: Then and now.* New Haven, CT: Yale University Press.

Quality education as a constitutional right: Creating a grassroots movement to transform public schools. Boston: Beacon Press.

Rist, R. (1970). Student social class and teacher expectation: The self-fulfilling prophecy of ghetto education. *Harvard Education Review, 40*(3), 411–54.

Rogers, C. (1961). *On becoming a person.* Boston: Houghton Mifflin.

Rosenthal, R., & Jacobson, L. (1968). *Pygmalion in the classroom.* New York: Holt, Rhinehart, and Winston.

Smrekar, C., & Goldring, E. (2009). Unitary status, neighborhood schools and re-segregation. In C. Smrekar & E. Goldring (Eds.). *From the courtroom to the classroom: The shifting landscape of school desegregation.* Cambridge, MA: Harvard Education Press.

Somers, C., & Pilawsky, M. (2004). Drop-out prevention among urban African American adolescents: Program evaluation and practical implications. *Preventing School Failure, 48*(3), 17–22.

Southern Education Foundation (2007). *A new majority: Low income students in the South's public schools.* From www.southerneducation.org.

Spring, J. (2007). *Deculturalization and the struggle for equality: A brief history of the education of dominated cultures in the United States.* New York: McGraw-Hill.

Steele, C. M., & Aronson, J. (1995). Stereotype threat and the intellectual performance of African Americans. *Journal of Personality and Social Psychology, 69*(5), 797–811.

Sue, D. W. (1981). *Counseling the culturally different: Theory and practice.* New York: John Wiley & Sons.

Thernstrom, A., & Thernstrom, S. (2003). *No excuses: Closing the racial gap in learning.* New York: Simon and Schuster.

Walker, V. (1996). *Their highest potential: An African American school community in the segregated South.* Chapel Hill: University of North Carolina Press.

Watkins, W. (2001). *The white architects of black education: Ideology and power in America, 1865–1954.* New York: Teachers College Press.

Wilkinson, R., & Pickett, K. (2009). *The spirit level: Why greater equality makes societies stronger.* New York: Bloomsbury Press.

Zimmerman, R., Khoury, E., Vega, W., Gil, A., & Warheit, G. (1995). Teacher and parent perceptions of behavior problems among a sample of African American, Hispanic, and non-Hispanic white students. *American Journal of Community Psychology, 23*(2), 181–97.

About the Author

Martha R. Bireda, Ph.D., has over twenty years of experience as an equity consultant specializing in issues related to race, gender, cultural diversity, and empowerment. The primary focus of her work is racial disparity in discipline and academic achievement. She has a broad background in education, which includes Head Start and Title I teaching, counseling, curriculum design, and program development. Dr. Bireda's "socially responsive pedagogy" conceptual framework is designed to assist in the restructuring of the culture and climate of low-performing schools serving predominately poor minority populations. Dr. Bireda is the author of *Cultures in Conflict: Eliminating Racial Profiling,* published by Rowman & Littlefield Education.